THE BARNS OF MAINE

THE BARNS OF MAINE

OUR HISTORY, OUR STORIES

DON PERKINS

THE
History
PRESS

Published by The History Press
Charleston, SC 29403
www.historypress.net

All images courtesy of the author except where noted.

First published 2012
Second printing 2013
Third printing 2014

ISBN 978-1-5402-0676-3

Library of Congress Cataloging-in-Publication Data

Perkins, Don, 1970-
The barns of Maine : our history, our stories / Don Perkins.
pages cm
Summary: "This book tells the story of Maine barns, as well as the Mainers who have worked in, worked on and even resided in Maine's barns"-- Provided by publisher.
ISBN 978-1-5402-0676-3
1. Barns--Maine. I. Title.
NA8230.P46 2012
725'.37209741--dc23
2012034050

Notice: The information in this book is true and complete to the best of our knowledge. It is offered without guarantee on the part of the author or The History Press. The author and The History Press disclaim all liability in connection with the use of this book.

To Sonya, for whom this work owes a great deal

CONTENTS

ACKNOWLEDGEMENTS

My utmost thanks to the following for providing their barns, stories and assistance for this project:

(in order of appearance)

The Timber Framers Guild
Jane Fox, Freeport
Freeport Historical Society
Tom and Diana Allen, Sebago
Bridgton Historical Society
David and Terry Gagnon, Denmark
Mike Deering, Saco
Lois Deering Starbird, Solon
Dan and Sarah Pierce, New Gloucester
George, Gene and Mary Lou Stacey, Hiram
Sally Williams, Hiram
Rick Gerrish, Milo
Milo Historical Society
Richard and Geraldine Anderson, Scarborough
Carmel Morin, New Gloucester
Ryan Tripp, New Gloucester
Garin and Sarah Smith, Skowhegan
Stephanie Calder, Skowhegan
Bob Bartlett (deceased), formerly of Oxford
Elizabeth Dominic, Searsport
Hank and Heidi Thorburn, Harpswell
Gail Hart, Harpswell
Peter, George and James Haines, Bethel
Randall, Jill and Allison Bates, New Vineyard
Dan and Claudia Sortwell, Wiscasset
Clarence and Juliet Plourde, Caribou
Dan Deveau, Cyr Plantation

ACKNOWLEDGEMENTS

Ken Arndt, Presque Isle

Shawn Michaud, Easton

Noah Yoder, Fort Fairfield

Granville "Peaunt" Perkins, Fort
Fairfield

John and Marie Dudley, Alexander

Richard Carlow, Wesley

Aaron Bell and Carly DelSignore,
Edmunds Township

Roger Knight, Scarborough

Jim Leary, Saco

George Hall, Windham

Jeremie Berube, Arundel

Scott Hatch, Harrison

Scott Burner, Windham

Mike Franck, Gorham

A very special thanks also goes out to those who backed this project on
Kickstarter and became "barn backers."

Joey Brunelle, San Francisco,
California

Angelo Castigliola, Biddeford,
Maine

Gene Cetrone, Rinebeck, New York

Bill and Ruth Crane, Windham,
Maine

John and Karen DenBleyker,
Millville, New Jersey

Tama Benson Donovan, Ipswich,
Massachusetts

Bob Fowler, New Gloucester, Maine

Donna Godfrey, Raymond, Maine

James Haines, Bethel, Maine

Sam Hotchkiss, Portland, Maine

Julie Jenkins, Bangor, Maine

Louise Knapp, Hebron, Maine

Caroline Loupe, New Gloucester,
Maine

Dave Martel, Saco, Maine

Paul and Nancy Michaud, Caribou,
Maine

Fabien and Brenda Pelletier,
Wallagrass, Maine

Deborah Perkins, Poland, Maine

Janine Pineo, Hudson, Maine

Bill Punsky, Cape Elizabeth, Maine

Andrew and Nina Roth-Wells,
Georgetown, Maine

Caroline Sample, Cumberland,
Maine

Susan Simonson, Westbrook, Maine

Wendy Smith, Windham, Maine

Daniel and Claudia Sortwell,
Wiscasset, Maine

Jeff Stanton, South Portland, Maine

Iain and Ada Dawn Stenhouse,
Poland, Maine

Jonathan Stern, San Diego,
California

Chandler Vreeland, Marietta,
Georgia

John Warden, Alexandria, Virginia

INTRODUCTION

Inotice them everywhere now, our barns, but it wasn't always that way. Like many lifelong Mainers, I almost certainly took these buildings for granted as much as anybody—they were just part of my everyday. But through years of examination, I have learned to appreciate the uniqueness and understand the richness that is a barn, especially the old New England barns of Maine.

It's hard to pinpoint exactly when it happened. The idea for this book started as a column in a local newspaper. Freelance writers often have to come up with their own material, and I was looking for something different to feature as a weekly series, something local and a bit unique. Why not barns?

As a carpenter and woodworker before becoming a writer, I knew I could draw on that experience. I have studied timber framing off and on now for twenty-plus years. Anything related to woodworking and done with hand tools has been a passion of mine since watching my grandfather apply his skills when I was young. And as a lifelong resident of Cumberland County, I knew where some of the old barns were. But that's all I had going for me.

At first, I feared there might be precious little to write about. This whole thing could backfire. "Barns?" people would say when I broached it, as if there couldn't possibly be anything interesting about the subject. But I received the go-ahead and set out on my first prospect: a big forty-four- by eighty-four-foot New England barn from the early 1800s.

I was hoping there would be stories to tell, and I found them, like the eighty-one-year-old man with the one-hundred-foot gambrel—one of the largest barns in the state. With just three cows in this mammoth barn, he lives alone and feeds them hay religiously each and every day. And then there is the one about the man who methodically restored his own barn. The building makes a great place to store the family's Model Ts—both father and son have one. He tells of double-planking the new floor, lining the space in between with silver coins and then joining his kids in signing their names on the inside faces of the planks. The rash of weather vane thefts in the 1980s—some of which reportedly employed helicopters—hit multiple barns and is a somewhat bizarre element I heard about often while visiting barns. And then there is the story of one farming family with a big old majestic barn beside their house. When their parents died, the children had the barn's image laser engraved on the family headstone. And on it goes.

For many, our barns are larger than life. The New England barn is an icon of the landscape, and Maine is fortunate to have retained many of them. Barns are huge repositories in both the literal and figurative senses. Their vast spaces have been filled with animals, experience and history. One farmer may own a barn, but those who grew up nearby or pass it each day on their way to work get something from it, too. They are symbols of rural community. In fact, barns may be one of humanity's oldest civic buildings.

That's why I've chosen to call them *our* barns. They're from a different time and can serve as symbols of stability in a world racked with change. Barns last for generations; they're honest buildings, built long before the days of plastic and plywood. Highly skilled artisans constructed them from local materials, both of which have become quite rare these days.

Barns awaken our senses. Their scale and romance can be alluring. They, like old trees we may have climbed as kids, can shelter more than mere hay and animals. They can be playgrounds for the soul, just like those big trees. You can escape in a barn.

Barns serve as a hub where many aspects of our rural past emanate: immigration patterns, lumber technology, obsolete professions, the challenges of the dairy industry and local economies are some of the spokes radiating out. There is much to discover about these buildings; they're filled with lore and will likely educate us for years to come.

For decades, barns have been largely under the radar and somewhat forgotten. Indeed, contrary to what one might think, barns are vast subjects. Much is unknown simply because they're from a different time. This is a point to be stressed. We are revisiting and discussing subjects that were hardly ever recorded in how we think of modern teachings today. Barns, both their origins and evolution, are from an oral history, from a time when much of the populace was neither literate nor numerate. Much like the apprenticed craftsmen who built them, they are from the old days, before consistent tape measures and standardized lumber sizes.

Sadly, most of the knowledge possessed by those old craftsmen died quietly with them. Today, small numbers of enthusiasts the world over pour over these aging structures like archaeologists (I like to call them "barnologists"), hoping to decipher the regional building practices that are as countless as they are mysterious. Barns are more than common farm buildings; they're testaments to our long agrarian history and the trades associated with it.

Despite the highly technical tone that can be coupled with writings on historic building practices, this book is intended for a general audience and is not meant to be a groundbreaking review of Maine's historic timber frame construction. It will be a departure from the paradigm of some barn books that have focused primarily on construction. These buildings have a richness that transcends this; they were worked and built by *people*. In this book, I will relay the words of those who have worked in our barns, as well as provide an overview of basic historic timber framing details, practices and terms found here in Maine. Along the way, the reader will find it of great benefit to consult the glossary at the back of this book for an explanation of uncommon terms regarding the many parts of a barn's frame as well as tools and associated methods. For example, a *bent* is a noun in this book and refers to a frame section or timber truss within a barn's skeletal structure. A bent runs transversely in a frame: one post rises to meet a beam, which follows to another post on the barn's opposite side. This truss is referred to as a bent.

What puzzled me in the initial days of researching our barns is just how little has been written about them. I thought a topic as common as barns would have been thoroughly researched, but this is not the case. What's more, finding a survey of Maine's barns proved to be even more difficult. We have largely taken them for granted and now race to learn more before heavy snows, fire and development claim more of these majestic old farm buildings.

Many things have been discovered through the writing of this book. The fact that Maine folks are proud of their barns is certainly one of them. Barn owners are a special crowd. And it's nice that even today, many of us still find barns in the network of our everyday experience. For me, finding barns to feature proved pretty straightforward. Many folks I associate with either own barns or know where the interesting ones are located. And owners seem to thoroughly enjoy the prospect of having their buildings celebrated. It's clear that many of you realize you have something special, and you do.

That we still have barns in good numbers is likely due to an age-old factor of life in the Pine Tree State: we are at the end of the line in terms of the rest of the nation. The tradition of Maine's slow progress is likely the silver lining that has preserved our barns and their surrounding environment. Moreover, Maine still has a functioning Shaker community, the last of its kind in the world. And the iconic log-drives—Maine held its last on the Kennebec River in 1976—are a nineteenth-century industrial practice that continued almost into the twenty-first century. Additionally, Southern Maine illustrates the flux of the late twentieth century perhaps better than any other part of the state. In the last thirty years, the malls and big box stores have come at a rapid pace, and suburban sprawl is certainly here, but two-hundred-year-old barns are still found in many of the shadows.

Development is but one factor threatening our barns. Farms everywhere are in decline, whether it be in Falmouth or Fairfield, simply because there are not enough members of the new generation either who want to or can farm. And heavy snow and fire knows no bounds. But thanks to rugged construction, old-growth timber and those who lovingly restore these structures, our barns have stood the test of time quite well and will no doubt continue to surprise, inspire and delight us.

CHAPTER ONE

EARLY BARNS

Traditional Structures Before the Civil War

ENGLISH BARNS

The first of the three basic generations or types of barn in Maine is the "English barn." It's what the colonists brought with them directly from England and where the roots of the word *barn* derive.

With its origins in grain, specifically barley, "barn" is an old English word from medieval times. It's why *barn* and *barley* share a common spelling. According to Webster's, the word barn is from the combination of the old English expressions for barley ("bere") and house or store ("aern"). Thus, barn is a name for a "barley house" or "barley store." In modern times, we may be surprised to learn the word has nothing to do with livestock whatsoever. The book *Memoirs of Odd Adventures, Strange Deliverances, etc., In the Captivity of John Gyles* (1736) recounts the capture and ensuing days of the garrison commander of the St. Georges River. There is a reference to a barn with nothing whatsoever to even suggest a building: "When we had gathered our corn and dried it, we put some into Indian barns; that is into holes in the ground, lined and covered with bark, and then with dirt."

It appears the word has a similar history with the French, who call a barn a *grange*. Rather than livestock, "grange" has its roots in grain storage and is from the medieval Latin word *granica*, which is from the Latin *granum*, or "grain."

English barns were the first type of barn in Maine. Plain and nearly devoid of features, these barns had few if any windows or ornamentation and were nearly always detached from the farmhouse. *Sketch by Philip E. Gagnon.*

The placement of the main entry doors, typically under the eaves side of the building, is what determines if a barn is an English barn. Because these old barns were principally designed for grain storage and processing, the farmer wanted his barn doors (front and rear) where the wind could blow through the shortest dimension of the building. Typically located at the building's center, these doors would open to reveal the threshing floor. Mows on either side held grain or hay.

Grain was the principal crop farmed in the early days of Maine's frontier. Wild game, the main source of meat, was plentiful in the nearby forests. As the years progressed, livestock was often kept on one side of the main aisle, away from an English barn's central threshing floor.

When the early farmer harvested his grain (be it barley, wheat or oats), he brought it to his English barn, where it was placed on the threshing floor and subsequently threshed (or thrashed)—that is, beaten with a flail, a tool consisting of two sticks joined by a short piece of leather or cord. The grain was beaten until its outer husk was broken, revealing the grain within. The term "to separate the wheat from the chaff" has its roots directly from the winnowing practice that followed. This step was typically carried out on a windy day. The farmer gathered up his flailed (beaten) grain and chaff from the threshing floor into a wide basket or tray, or perhaps two people would cradle it in a blanket. The threshing floor was then swept clean. Standing in the middle of the threshing floor with the barn doors open wide, the farmer then tossed his mixture up toward the barn ceiling. If everything went as planned, the rush of wind slicing through the barn would carry off the lighter chaff while the heavier grain was allowed to fall back to the floor. What stopped the grain from blowing out of the barn entirely was the threshold. (Many will recognize the term "threshold," as in "he carried the new bride over the threshold," suggesting the wooden board at the base of a doorway. This is another of many terms taken directly from the history of our barns.)

MY DREAM HOUSE: FREEPORT

Jane Fox never knew she lived with a direct link to the old world, but she does. Her barn on Freeport's Flying Point Road has its roots in medieval England. Measuring thirty-two by forty feet, it's a classic English barn: small, with main entry doors on the eaves side and possessing few adornments. The whole barn has but four windows; there's no fancy trim detail anywhere. It's inside where the art lies.

Fox bought the property in 1978 and calls the homestead "her dream house." While living in Arizona some years ago, the Hampden native planned a return to Maine but wanted just the right place. She gave her realtor a specific list of criteria. "I wanted a house with an attached barn and some acreage," Fox said. "A little while later, this is where we ended up."

With twenty-eight acres, Freeport elders will know this as the Randall Farm. One longtime Freeport resident told her that Flying Point Road originally went behind the barn.

"They didn't build farmhouses this far back from the road," Fox said, gesturing to where Flying Point Road is today.

As is often the case, an exact date for the barn is unknown. Details point to an early era, likely late 1700s to early 1800s. The barn's frame

The joinery inside this Freeport English barn displays direct connections to medieval England.

is completely hand-hewn (that is, processed by hand with axes). Even the smaller pieces, including the braces, are hewn. There are some who say a barn with hewn braces will predate the first sawmill, but this is a theory heavily influenced on locality. Not all of my visits to barns in the Pine Tree State support this. It is true that most old barns will at least have sawn bracing when the rest of the frame is hewn, so it's worth noting when an old barn in a prominent coastal town like Freeport would exhibit a completely hand-hewn frame.

Another early indicator is the presence of the English tying joint, a section of the frame where the post top, wall plate and rafter intersect. This is where the artistry of the medieval world manifests in Freeport, Maine. The English tying joint begins with a tapered or flared post (sometimes referred to as a jowled post), one that begins square at the bottom and fattens ever wider toward its top to provide the extra surface area needed for the rest of the frame's major intersecting members. As such, the English tying joint "tied" the frame together in a very effective manner. The roots of the jowled post date back to thirteenth-century England. In fact, the oldest barns left standing in the world are The Barley and Wheat Barns at Cressing Temple in Essex. The Wheat Barn (circa 1250) exhibits jowled posts. Built by the Knights Templar, this barn measures 41 by 131 feet and has an oak frame made from the wood

An English tying joint is located at the top of this post, the section where post top, wall plate and rafter intersect.

of some 472 oak trees. Its aisle posts are flared and notched at the top to accept a continuous top plate, much like the posts here at the barn on Flying Point Road. The English tying joint was perfected and became the standard in barn building for some five hundred years, continuing to flourish in New England.

Fox never farmed here but kept two horses that she remembers fondly. In 2009, the barn started to show its age; one wall on the gable end had significant rot. Fox toyed with the idea of selling the property and moving to Brunswick where she works as an interior designer. She contacted a realtor and had the property appraised.

"This wall of the barn was in terrible shape," Fox recalled. "I said to the realtor, 'do you think I should repair that before the house goes on the market?'"

The answer she got was a surprise and a sad revelation.

"'Anyone who buys this is going to tear the barn down right away,'" Fox said, summarizing the realtor's remarks.

In an English tying joint, a "jowled" (or flared) post gets wider at its top to provide surface area for intersecting joinery. An upside down "VI" can be seen pairing two timbers together.

Owner Jane Fox stands with historic carpenters Heidi and Hank Thorburn.

Fox took stock of these words and ultimately decided not to sell in a down market. She quickly decided to have the barn repaired, contacting a historic housewright from Harpswell.

"Now I like it even more," she said. "I feel I have a responsibility to save this barn."

Many are glad she did, as it is likely one of Freeport's oldest remaining barns. The design of the English barn is evident whenever the doors are thrown open. A brisk wind whips through the center that would have nicely assisted a farmer's threshing chores years ago.

"I don't ever have to sweep the floor," Fox said.

THE NEW ENGLAND BARN EMERGES

New Englanders are nothing if not innovative. Following the English barn, the first barn style that appeared in Maine, Yankees soon developed their own style and established what's generally referred to as the New England or "Yankee" barn. By moving the entrance from the eaves wall to the gable end, farmers found a new design that was better suited to a new land with a different climate that required different farming practices. With a long central aisle, this second-generation barn is what most of us in Maine recognize when we think "barn."

Two things, as indicated, drove a change in barn-entry design among the English in America: climate and farming practices. Where grain had been the driver of barn layout in the Old World, raising livestock became more common in New England. Maine was no exception.

Historic study often reveals the real story of what happened in a given era and time. Contrary to our romantic notions, most of Maine has never been great farmland. Rocky soil abounds. Most of the state raised stonewalls before any other crop, and our growing season is far too short. In truth, farming never really drew anyone to the Pine Tree State at all, at least in America's early years. It was lumber and fishing that brought most people here, and this is precisely why most of Maine's population sprung up in the form of coastal villages or mill sites located on rivers and streams.

During the Civil War, many Maine boys literally saw greener pastures in places like Ohio. They would relocate in droves, leaving abandoned barns and failed farms in their wake. In *Farming in Maine* (1954), Clarence Day quotes the 1889 agriculture secretary, Z.A. Gilbert:

> *"These abandoned farms should never have been cleared." Why then were they? Many a man has wondered about that as he stood among the bushes "where once a garden smiled," or viewed the little, odd-shaped, boulder-strewn fields where nothing but hawkweed grew.*

But, of course, whenever a courageous family or lumberman did venture into the wilds of early Maine, folks needed to survive, and farms and barns naturally sprang up to fill this need. Besides draft animals, the first livestock appears to have been sheep. Beef cattle were also common. It would be several decades if not a century (well after the Civil War) before dairy

A New England barn stands at Shaker Village in New Gloucester. The new design, which features the main entrance at the gable end instead of the eaves wall, was better suited to a new land where climate and farming practices were different.

assumed any type of prominence for the family farmer. Thus, the increased practice of keeping livestock made larger barns necessary.

With its main entry along the eaves wall, the English barn proved difficult to expand. It was easy enough to add on to, but these expanded buildings proved inefficient. Adding to the left or right of an English barn increases the distance from the main aisle, making serviceability with a horse and wagon increasingly difficult. Expanding to the rear of an English barn diminishes the sloping roofline. Somewhere in time, a farmer had a realization: if he moved the entry to the gable end and then aligned the main aisle with the roof ridge and ran this the full length of the structure with an exit door at the other end, all areas of the building could be serviced. Expansion was as easy as adding a bent or two at the end. The building's layout remained the same, the farmer just got a longer version of the original Yankee barn design.

Upon inspection, you'll find that many early New England or Yankee barns are actually two English-style barns that were dragged together and placed end to end. New siding, roofing and an entrance and exit were then

A closer look inside a Harpswell barn reveals this is really two buildings that have been moved together. Notice the pair of posts right next to each other. On either side of these posts, subtle differences can be seen in nearly every aspect of the two buildings.

constructed at each gable to make these configurations appear as if they were always one building.

The New England climate was also influential in the development of new barn designs. In England, it snows but only a fraction of what a Maine winter typically dishes out. In Maine, farmers discovered they needed to keep both their animals, crops and hay sheltered for largely half of the year. This required a larger barn. Additionally, with the main entry moved to the gable end, depositing rain and snow was also diverted from the main entry where it had previously soaked the farmer as he went in and out. It also eroded the immediate traffic area. The new design worked exceptionally well for the burgeoning New England farmer.

An Isolated Slice of a Past Preserved: Sebago

Some barns are connected to the house, some are separated by a few feet and still others are located across the road entirely. Such is the case on Sebago's Peaked Mountain Road, a dirt lane slicing through a pastoral and isolated section of town. For over a century, not much has changed here. The first time I saw this barn was by sheer happenstance. Trying to get to Hiram from the western side of Sebago Lake, I followed what looked like the shortest route on the map. But it turned out to be the long way. The road was rough, and I had to go slow, and the suspension on my car suffered. I'm glad I took that route, however, because while heading west, I crested a hill and soon found myself rubbernecking at a beautiful cedar-shingled barn with a bright red roof that was standing all by itself. I didn't stop as I was pressed for time, but I made sure to write the location down. I later discovered that this barn belongs to former congressional

This circa 1840 detached barn belongs to former Congressman Tom Allen.

representative Tom Allen, who served from 1996–2008. Allen's parents purchased this farm in 1951. It includes about 175 acres today.

"The reason my parents bought this place was because my grandparents bought a farm on the nearby Convene Road in 1923," Allen said. "My father and his five siblings spent time over there; I think my father wanted to replicate that experience."

It was the Boothby family who were the first on this parcel. Allen has documents that state the land was deeded in 1843 to Arthur Boothby by William Fitch. It's thought that Boothby built the farmhouse and barn around 1846. His name appears beside a square representing a dwelling on an old 1857 Cumberland County map.

Construction details in the barn suggest it was built prior to the Civil War. The foremost indicators are a hand-hewn frame of jowled posts that are topped by English tying joints. As aforementioned, the English tying joint dates back to the thirteenth century and is a marvel of joincry, carrying out its principal role of preventing roof spread with beauty as well as utility for well over two hundred years after it first appeared in New England barns. For something to last that long, it must have worked very well indeed.

Because they own an old barn, the Allens attended a talk I gave at the Bridgton Historical Society and became intrigued upon discovering the history of the English tying joint and its connection to their own barn. They had little knowledge that the construction lineage traced back to medieval England, or that the joint held such long-standing tradition with the English. Armed with this newfound knowledge, the Allens recently traveled to England for a book fair and decided to take a side trip to see the great tithe barns at Cressing Temple—the origins of the joinery in their own barn.

"The wood in these barns is centuries old," Tom said upon his return. "It looks as if the air has kind of eaten away at them. You get a feeling of time; almost eight centuries have passed."

The English tying joint began with the medieval jowled post and reappeared in barn configurations in Maine for almost six centuries. It's significant to consider the long run this joint configuration had; few things have enjoyed such a tenure.

"To think that the joinery in our barn, [which was] built in the 1840s, goes back six hundred years is absolutely amazing," Tom said.

Knowing this, a greater context naturally arises when one enters old barns in Maine, and the buildings begin to tell their stories. What put an end to

A jowled post and English tying joint can be seen in this nearly two-hundred-year-old timber frame. Vertical wall boarding and a purlin roof system are common in early to mid-nineteenth-century barns in southern Maine.

Located inside one of the oldest barns left standing on Earth, this jowled post is an early version of the "English tying joint." Dating to approximately 1270, the "Wheat Barn" still stands in Essex, England, and was originally built by the Knights Templar. *Courtesy of Tom and Diana Allen.*

jowled posts and the English tying joint was essentially the advent of evenly-squared, sawmilled timber, a commodity that became evermore available following the Civil War when railroads helped transport large items. Though a builder could certainly still hand hew a tapered post with a couple of different axes if he so desired, the labor involved in such an activity—not to mention the complicated joinery at the post's top where multiple members come together—typically found a builder going with a ready-made square post right from the sawmill.

"Jowled post" is a term applied to a few different styles of wall posts that start out more or less square at their base and flare ever wider toward the top. Among the more common varieties is the "gunstock" style, which can be found in many old homes. The posts at Allen's barn start out roughly eight inches square at their base and flare ever wider in one direction, measuring about eight by twelve inches at the top. The added surface area of the jowled post is necessary to provide enough

Tom Allen stands beside one of the mammoth oak posts inside the medieval, thirteenth-century "Wheat Barn" in Essex, England. *Courtesy of Tom and Diana Allen.*

wood for the complicated joinery at a major joint intersection. The post top, rafter and wall plate all join here. These posts are large timbers. Because of their tapered geometry, jowled posts cannot be easily sawn, and thus, hand hewing lent itself perfectly to the job. A carpenter from the earlier days used the natural taper of a tree to his advantage when forming these posts. Essentially, a tree was inverted, and the butt of the tree, the wider section, would be oriented to become the post's top. Two perpendicular tenons were carved out: one was for the wall plate, which ran parallel to the building, and the other was set at ninety degrees a bit farther up the post where the tie beam intersected. The top of the post was notched to allow the continuous wall plate to pass through it. These plates often measure eight inches square. In this particular case, the extra four inches of jowled surface also provides a partial bearing for the tie beams, which support the major roof rafters. Besides hand-hewn timber and English tying joints, the Allens' barn displays a purlin roof system clad with vertical boarding. The walls are also sheathed in this vertical approach.

When first exploring barns, I was often puzzled by the appearance of different roof frames and boarding styles; some barns had purlin roof systems (where boarding is laid vertically), while others had common rafters with boarding affixed horizontally. Through a combination of research and my own experience, I discovered that vertical roof boarding is the dominant type in the southern half of Maine, roughly south of a line extending from Rangeley to Old Town and over to Eastport. Vertical boarding is also evident in most parts of New Hampshire, the eastern half of Vermont and most of eastern Massachusetts. Common rafter systems (where boarding is horizontal) are the dominant style found everywhere else in New England, including the northern half of Maine. Thomas Durant Visser goes into more detail in his book *Field Guide to New England Barns and Farm Buildings* (1997):

> *To understand why there are such regional variations* [of construction], *settlement patterns in the diffusion of influence from the cultural centers of colonial New England should be considered.*
>
> *In colonial New England two primary population centers developed around Massachusetts Bay and Connecticut. After immigrants from various locations in England established these colonies between the 1620s and the 1640s, a short period of inland settlement was halted by almost a century and a half of intermittent wars. As the hostilities brought relative isolation to the colonies, they gradually established their own cultural identities, based partly on the traditions brought from the English homelands and partly on the group's own innovations, adaptations, and exposure to new influences.*

There are others in the historic timber framing community who propose yet another element: What was the intended roofing material, wood shingles or simply boards? Wood shingles necessitate a substrate of horizontal strapping as a nailing surface, whereas a "board roof" of simply vertically applied boards—perhaps comprised of overlapping layers or battens covering the seams between—would be fastened to a network of horizontal purlins. Old photographs often feature these simple board roofs on outbuildings. Another aspect to consider is the proficiency of the builder. A common rafter system, such as is practiced today on modern house construction, takes less skill to construct than its purlin counterpart. As I ventured into barn study, I learned the picture grows even more varied: Some roof systems can contain a combination of both rafter *and* purlin systems. Roofs are some of the most interesting and intricate parts of a barn's construction.

The Allens' barn is a wonderful example of the ease at which a New England barn could be expanded. The efficiency of the design is readily apparent. Originally measuring forty by forty feet, a common size for a beginning farmer, the Allens' barn was almost doubled in size to seventy feet. It's not certain when this was done, but based on the fact the addition is framed in almost the exact same manner (that is, with hand-hewn timber and English tying joints), it was likely soon after its initial construction and likely before the Civil War. Indeed, you would have to be well educated in barn construction to recognize it was added to at all.

There is one detail that sticks out and helps differentiate the two sections. In the original segment, at their base, the major rafters above each post are spiked clear through into the tie beam below with a trunnel, sometimes referred to as a "treenail," a long wooden spike that is usually $1\frac{1}{2}$ to 2 inches in diameter and pointed at one end. Bents one through five in the Allens' barn have trunnels, while the next three bents (the addition) do not. Hardware is uncommon in barns of the early 1800s; its expense and difficulty of procurement typically made it prohibitive. This is why everything is pegged in an old barn. The only hardware is usually its door hinges or rolling track. Even nails were used sparingly.

Boothby must have prospered between the 1840s and '50s to the point where he needed a larger building. With the beauty of the New England barn design, he simply added three more bents and nearly doubled his barn. In the twentieth century, many lean-to-like additions were built that surround the building on two sides.

In 1859, Boothby deeded the property to Herman Wight. The property stayed in the Wight family for two more generations. Whether Boothby or Wight specifically expanded the barn is lost to history, but it was likely Boothby. Why trunnels were not used is part of the mystery that makes barn research so interesting. There is always a detective story.

Despite the need for expansion early on, farming on any scale appears to have ended here soon after it began. Like a snapshot in time, there are many old relics left in the barn—not items of value but rather indicators that farming on a serious scale didn't last particularly long nor was it ever resurrected to its former glory. Leather hinges still hold some interior doors to their frame. Was it the Civil War that sent many able-bodied men off to fight or did the Wight family simply find it difficult to prosper as the Boothbys did? Whatever the case, many Maine farms changed after the Civil War. The railroads, which had helped the Union army in their battles with the Confederates, further linked the nation. Crops from the Midwest shipped via railcars put increasing competition on Maine farmers. Diverse family operations that were the norm of early farms gave way to increasing specialization after the Civil War. Commercialization in a certain crop or product was beginning to emerge.

The Allen property remains isolated even today; most of the road still lacks electricity. During winter, the Allens must arrive via snowshoes, skis or snowmobile as the whole road in not plowed. The barn is wired, however, as is the farmhouse across the street.

"Sometime in the twentieth century, a generator was put in that little building beside the road," Allen said. "The generator still works, but a few years ago I decided to install solar power. But the barn hasn't been powered since the 1940s."

Allen and his wife Diana love having history around them. The barn stands as a living testament to life in the area's bygone days.

"It's old," Allen said. "The history of a barn like this is obvious. You can see where the animals were, and you can get an idea of what kind of life was going on here. That's harder to see in a house. Houses tend to be updated. When you're in a barn like this, it's almost like you can see the past."

"When I walk in the barn, my imagination gets going," Diana said. "I've always had an affinity for old places."

Rather than use it as a year-round residence, the Allens use the home as a seasonal retreat. When he was a kid, Allen romped around the barn with his brothers and sisters. The building felt larger than life.

"We would run and jump down into some old hay," he said. "It was old, loose hay. It was dusty. We had a swing in there hanging from a big crossbeam, a big swing, and there was an old wagon and a buggy."

One time, Allen and his younger siblings got in the wagon and headed down the road.

"We started going down the hill, and I realized we were going too fast; I wasn't strong enough to hold it back," he said. "I jumped out and left them to their fate."

According to Allen, everyone made out just fine.

Early Barns

Diana and Tom Allen beside their New England barn in the town of Sebago.

Allen first came here in the early 1950s when he was six years old, and he recalled watching the fields being hayed when he was a boy. "Vernie Gregory and his sons Donald and Elroy would mow the fields with an old tractor," he said. "They took the loose hay in an old hayrack pulled by oxen and headed down the road."

According to Allen, Elroy, now in his eighties, still lives down the road in the house he was born in. He does not have a telephone.

Aside from being faithfully maintained, it is the barn's isolation here that has worked to preserve it in its original setting. Allen said that this house was the only one on the road until about 1970. There were also some derelict and abandoned homes around that time that have since been reclaimed by nature.

"In the last twenty years, there have been homes built on either side," he said, "but it's still very isolated. Compared to changes in the rest of the world, this road is pretty much like it was."

And Allen doesn't see things changing very much—at least that's his hope. Perhaps many would welcome the addition of modern conveniences like street power, but the lack of public utility service is what's helped slow the progress of time. I asked Allen if he thought telephone poles and lines were coming. He simply said, "I hope not."

BUILT UPON TEMPERANCE: BRIDGTON

What do you suppose the beverage on hand was in the days when communities built big barns? History says it was a barrel of rum, the traditional accompaniment to nearly each and every barn raising. However, one New Englander broke with tradition. Instead of raising his glass, George Fitch decided to raise his barn without liquid spirits.

In South Bridgton, the Bridgton Historical Society owns and maintains an early New England hilltop farmstead called "Narramissic," a Native American word meaning "hard to find." Its original settler was George Fitch's father-in-law, William Peabody, the son of a deacon. Peabody marched on Bunker Hill during the Revolution and arrived in Bridgton from Massachusetts in the mid-1780s. He initially lived nearby on land owned by his uncle, Enoch Perley. Apparently, religion (and sobriety) was an important driver in Mr. Peabody's life. The First Congregational Church of Bridgton was founded in the Peabody home on August 26, 1784.

In 1797, Peabody built a barn and erected the Narramissic farmstead on land beside his uncle. That first barn has been lost to time, but the beautiful barn that is here today was built in the early 1830s by William's son-in-law, George Fitch. And not a drop of rum was tasted upon its raising nor upon its completion.

Like their Peabody forebears, the Fitches were upright individuals. In *Ninety Years of Living*, Edwin Fitch (1840–1931), George Fitch's son, left a wonderful account of days at this farm. He describes his barn-building father as "[A man] of Puritan descent and true to his faith...Father was scrupulously upright. He did not understand the very young. But before he passed on, we did understand and love each other."

It's hard to emphasize the importance of religion felt by the populace in those early days. Despite the separation of church and state endowed by the Constitution in 1787, in the early years of New England, a church was often mandated in order to incorporate a town. It's also worth

Early Barns

The Temperance Barn, built circa 1830 in Bridgton, is so named because not a drop of rum, the traditional accompaniment at nineteenth-century barn raisings, was had. Notice the offset door, which is a common feature on pre–Civil War Maine barns.

noting that the Prohibition era had its roots in the temperance movement that started in Portland, Maine. Even today, as we approach the 100th anniversary of prohibition's repeal, the Pine Tree State still has a few "dry towns" in its midst.

It's worth mentioning a few accounts of building tradition, many of which apparently involved imbibing. In *History of the Lumber Industry of America* (1907), James Elliott Defebaugh describes the construction of early sawmills in the Bangor area along the Penobscot River:

> *Other mills followed in rapid succession, and the erection of each, like the raising of a barn in the good old days, was made the occasions of a general celebration with "liquid features." Of the erection of one of these Eighteenth Century mills, history states: "they got the mill up the first of the winter and used two puncheons and one barrel of New England rum and had not enough liquor to finish the raising and completing the mill.*

About thirty miles to the southeast of the Temperance Barn is the 1807 Portland Observatory, the only known marine signaling tower left in the nation. If you take a tour of the structure anytime between Memorial Day to Columbus Day and view the heavy timbers within, you'll hear about how workers had regular "rum breaks" every day they were on the job.

Another account recorded in Josiah Howard Temple's and George Sheldon's *A History of the Town of Northfield, Massachusetts* (1875) describes a house-raising in Northfield, Massachusetts: "The stone for the foundations of the new house were drawn and laid, and the frame raised in the early part of the summer. To supply the requirements of the 'raising,' the committee purchased 2 barrels of New England rum...and 4 gallons of West India rum."

Raisings of any and all types were important affairs, especially in early communities. Sometimes there was a shortage of manpower, and others were enlisted for heavy lifting, as described in another passage in Defebaugh's history:

> *About 1780 Daniel Hill, Jermiah Frost and Jacob Libbey built a small, rude mill. It stood on Porter's Stream* [near Calais], *near its mouth, and was the first mill ever erected in this vicinity. The number of men at the "raising" was so small that the ladies were obliged to lend all their strength in lifting the heavy timbers. Without their aid the frame could not have been set up.*

The Temperance Barn measures forty by sixty feet, a very common size for a nineteenth-century barn in Maine. It was built in the old way and reflects the English lineage of the region, having flared posts and English tying joints. The frame was constructed via the scribe rule. Roman numerals are at all prominent joint locations. The barn is completely separate from the house and is a New England barn, having a gable-entry, center-aisle design. It also has an offset entry door, which indicates it is a pre–Civil War barn. And it's a well-built one at that. Crafted from eight- by eight-inch timbers, six bents that are spaced on twelve-foot centers make up the frame. The top plates along each of the eaves are continuous, the timbers measuring some sixty feet long, and are slightly larger in cross section than the rest of the frame.

Like all offset-aisle, gable-entry barns in the region, livestock was kept on the south-facing side in the narrow section of the barn, which is just to

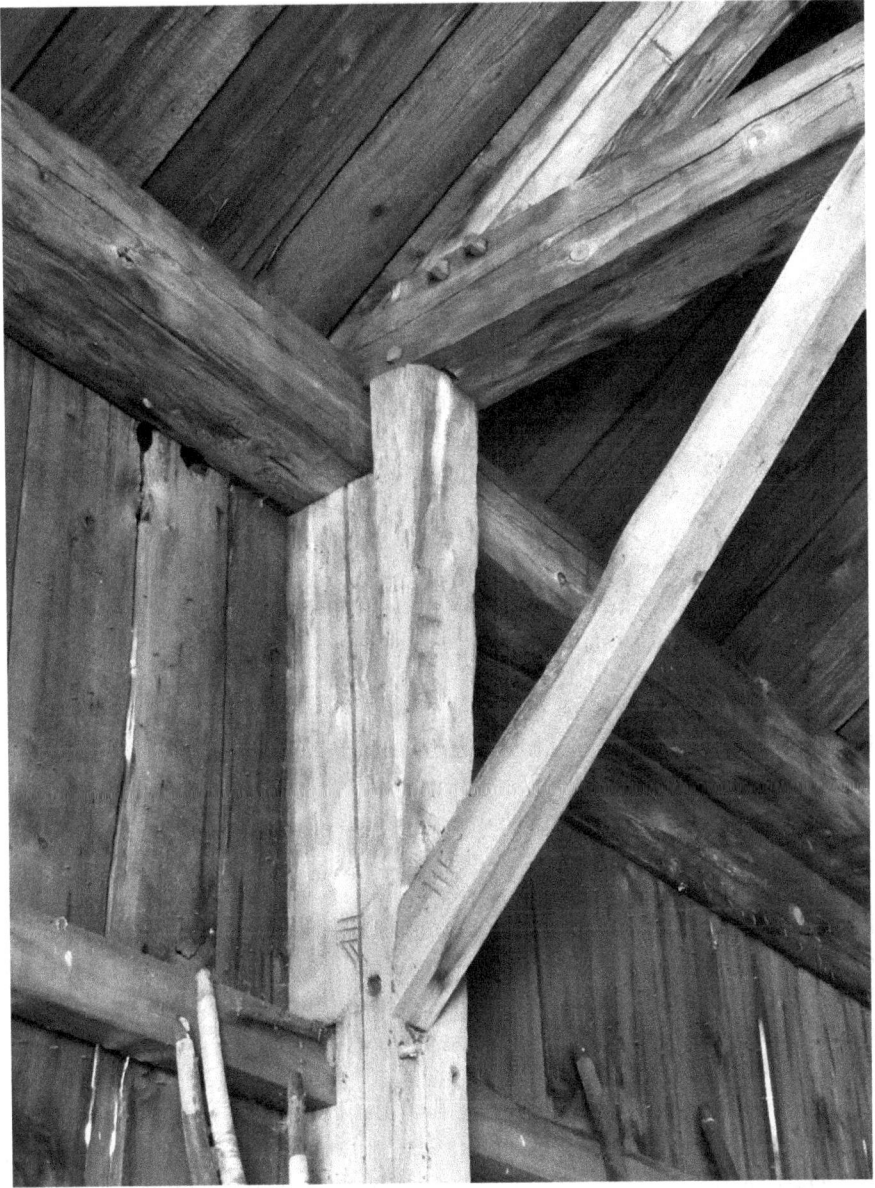

English tying joints and a hand-hewn frame within the Temperance Barn, which belongs to the Bridgton Historical Society. Note the carpenter's marks chiseled into both the brace and post.

the left of the main entryway. This area is twelve feet wide, and the center aisle is also twelve feet wide. The haymow along the north-facing wall is the largest section of the floor plan, measuring sixteen feet in width. Like most Maine farms before the Civil War, this one had diverse operations. Specialization in a certain crop or commodity had not yet made its way into the formula of the region. In *Ninety Years of Living*, Fitch writes, "Father believed in diversified farming, therefore we had a flock of sheep, milch cows, pigs, chickens and geese."

Fitch states that tea, coffee, sugar and salt were the only items necessary to purchase. Clothes were made at home directly from wool. The family had two apple orchards that brought in a suitable income (Baldwin apples reportedly made the best money for this Bridgton farm). It may be surprising to many today to learn that, in the 1850s, an apple orchard was the best source of income for the Maine farmer, according to Clarence Day's *A History of Maine Agriculture 1604–1860.* (Dairy was still a few decades away from becoming a major source of income for farm families.) In 1850, the Fitch family not only grew apples but also pears, grapes, cherries and plums, corn, oats, peas and beans. Three hundred bushels of potatoes rounded out things nicely. Fifty tons of hay was recorded in an 1850 agricultural census of what the farm had on hand. Livestock included two horses, six milch (the old English spelling for milk) cows, four oxen, six other cattle, sixteen sheep and one hog. Many of these animals were no doubt kept in the barn, which would have made it a virtual bank for a family of eleven in those days.

"Although we lived in cold and sterile Maine, we did not lack for many luxuries of life," Edwin wrote. Edwin also described how the attic provided a place for children to play, as they were not allowed to play inside the main house in those days. "The attic was one vast room where we youngsters were monarchs of all we surveyed," wrote Edwin. "When the weather would not permit us to stay outdoors we had great times here."

The barn was another place free from the constraints of instilled order found within the proper rooms of the family home. If a young boy were to kiss a girl, he had a much better chance doing so in the barn, especially when the corn was ready.

> *After corn harvesting came husking. It was the custom in those days to fill the barn floor with unhusked corn, and then ask the young people to come in and husk it. We all enjoyed these occasions, a regular lark...many of our neighbors made a Gala event of it, asking all the girls to be there and help*

get the husking out of the way early so dancing could begin. There was a rule that whoever found a red ear was entitled to a kiss. There was some rivalry among the boys when they selected partners. Some of the girls would hide their red ears if their partner was not to their liking.

Fun on the farm was soon to change, however. At age sixteen, Edwin experienced an incident that altered the course of the farm in a significant way. One winter, while his father was out getting wood with oxen and a sled, the sled struck a dead tree by the side of the road and the top of it came down and hit his father on the head. It was thought that he received a concussion, and everyone assumed Edwin's father would recover. However, Edwin described coming home one day only to learn that was no longer the case. "One afternoon," he wrote, "when I came from school I rushed into his bedroom and saw at a glance that he was very much worse. No one spoke to me. I saw for myself that he had only a few hours to live."

What did poor Edwin do when faced with this dreadful insight? With the attic, blacksmith shop and surrounding woods and fields readily available, Edward chose to make a beeline for the barn.

"I immediately went out to the barn, climbed on top of the haymow and laid down and give way to the greatest grief that I have ever known. I cried until there were no more tears to fall. I had never known before how much I had loved my father."

The fact that Edwin saw the barn as an innate place of comfort is notable. After all, the barn sheltered the very essentials necessary to sustain the family. Perhaps Edwin felt it was also the only place that could harbor his powerful grief.

When living, George Fitch, the upright and teetotaling New Englander, was also an able and clever man. He possessed necessary carpentry skills. Edwin described how his father cut trees and hewed all the necessary timber to construct a blacksmith shed that still stands on the property today. The boards came from pine logs his father hauled to the sawmill. It's likely the Temperance Barn was made in a similar fashion. Its frame is composed of hand-hewn timber, and the vertical boarding is tongue-and-groove. This "matching" of boards was done to try and create a tight barn and keep out the rain and wind. Old barns were often not shingled; clapboards weren't used until later and often only on the front-facing or "public" sides of outbuildings. The vertical wall and roof boards display straight saw marks from a water-powered mill. Many are twenty inches wide.

A few years into its life, this barn was jacked eight feet into the air with a homemade wooden jackscrew and set upon a bed of split granite. The stone was quarried right on the property.

Edwin described more of his father's ingenuity in recounting how the barn was raised again, that is, after the whole building had been standing. "Later," he wrote, "either for a change or just for something to do, he decided to raise the larger barn to 8 feet. It already stood on 2 feet of underpinning of long strips of split stone."

As the barn was initially built on relatively flat land, it's likely that it was raised for a worthwhile purpose, most likely to provide a manure basement. These basements were becoming quite popular in the two decades following the barn's construction. The clever Yankee lifted his barn by making his own jack out of a hardwood log.

Father had made, out of hardwood, a screw of sufficient power to raise a building larger than our barn. He took a timber, enough to make a screw six inches in diameter, to a place where there was a turning lathe. Father had a lathe of his own, but it was too small. The rounded timber taken from the lathe had still to be made into a screw. The machine to do this was a metal screw with a knife attached, which went down through a hole in a metal plate and at every turn of this screw the knife went one inch lower. After the spiral was completed the process was repeated until the groove was deep enough. The nut for the screw was made the same way, only father made the hole with a large auger and then made it smooth and with his machine cut the grooves that corresponded to the screw. With this device he raised one side of the barn to the required height, having previously propped the other side with timbers so it would not slip off. Then, with an improvised derrick, proceeded to raise the stones and slip them into place. This is just one of the things he could do.

What a sight this must have been. One would guess Fitch would need several of these "screws" to lift a barn that was sixty feet long, but the account makes it sound like he did it with just one. This inspires many questions: Did he have any help? How did he turn the "nut" of this wooden jackscrew? Did the mechanism require any lubrication? How long did all of this take? Did he come up with this homemade raising tool himself or learn of it elsewhere? In any case, it's clear he did not go into this considerable, and what some might see as an utterly risky, pursuit simply for "something to do." The motivator was a manure basement. Earthen ramps were subsequently built at both the entryway and exit. As Edwin described, the farm was not lacking storage space: "It is needless to say that we never filled both barns to their capacity."

As the account states, raising one side and tilting the barn would have produced considerable stress on the building. However, the barn is well built and integrates sufficient bracing for the racking a lift would have caused. Unlike modern buildings that are sheathed in plywood (which cannot be easily sheared out of shape), timber-framed buildings need sufficient bracing that is mortised and pegged within the frame's structure. Rather than having short, lateral bracing at each post, the Temperance Barn has long, continuous bracing at the corners that begin toward the top of each post and follow down to connect with the sill plate several feet down the side of the building.

The building may have experienced the addition of a manure basement, but it never received much attention as far as ventilation. There is no cupola, another indication of an early nineteenth-century barn. The importance of ventilating a building was discovered after the manure basement was incorporated into barn design and was especially handy in humid conditions, as described in an 1852 issue of *New England Farmer.*

> *The breath from cattle, together with the vapor rising from the manure, which defies all attempts to keep it below the floor if the cellar is warm, covers, not only the floor over the cellar, but the beams, and the whole underside of the roof, with pearly trickling drops for weeks together during the winter. If the doors are thrown open in order to evaporate this moisture, you lose the benefits you have been seeking in making a tight barn, by reducing the temperature so much that cattle require more food, while the effect is to reduce the flow of milk in the cows. Many large and valuable barns have been very much damaged by being placed over a manure cellar without proper ventilation.*

The Fitch family and its descendants owned the property until the 1930s. Edwin went off to fight for the Union during the Civil War and was taken prisoner but survived to return home. Records indicate that he did not farm the property. This task would fall largely to the family's women. Unfortunately, beginning with the passing of Edwin's father and Edwin's subsequent military enlistment, the farm never repeated its earlier successes.

The name Narramissic was given to this property in the twentieth century by Margaret Monroe, its fifth owner. She purchased it in 1938 for $1,250 in back taxes. It appears the Great Depression was the final blow for the original family. The Bridgton Historical Society states that the name Narramissic was given not to depict its isolation but to reflect the fact that Monroe and her husband had searched far and wide for the perfect property before ultimately deciding to settle here. Sadly, Monroe found herself a widow by the time she finally got to the old farm, which she visited only seasonally in the warmer months. Prior to her ownership, the farm remained within the Peabody-Fitch family and was passed down through its maternal side for some 140 years. It never received plumbing or electricity until Mrs. Monroe's tenure in the late 1930s. In 1988, Monroe willed it to the historical society, which has operated it as a museum ever since.

When the society acquired the building, the late Bob Dunning, an expert in timber frame restoration, put in many hours shoring up the barn and replacing its rotted elements. More recently, a new barn roof has been installed. As any barn owner knows, maintaining these buildings can prove a considerable expense today. The society raised nearly $28,000 for a new metal roof and some further sill repair. A new roof is a wonderful line of defense that should ensure this superbly preserved barn stands for many decades to come.

A Shift in Timber Frame Technology: Denmark

In the town of Denmark, under the shadow of Pleasant Mountain and not very far from Bridgton's Temperance Barn, sits a wonderful barn on Hio Ridge Road. At first glace, the eighty-foot barn, built circa 1835, may look nice and uniform, but upon closer inspection, its design shows a distinct and important shift in barn-building technology. Sometime after 1860, three bents were added to the rear of this building, nearly doubling the barn's length. We know this based on the joinery.

Though the entire building is framed more or less in the same manner—with hand-hewn timber and consistent boarding arrangements throughout—there are several details that point to a subtle yet significant change. The major joint intersections at the front of the barn display roman numerals. These are the telltale signs of the "scribe rule" method

In Denmark, Maine, old and new owners in front of the barn that ties them together. *From left to right*: Mike Deering, Terry Gagnon, Lois Deering Starbird and David Gagnon.

where everything was custom fitted, marked and paired together. After the barn's fifth bent, however, the marriage marks end; little flat areas called "housings" can be seen chiseled into the hand-hewn timbers. Also, there is a noticeable alteration in the braces: the saw marks from where they were milled are visible.

Water-powered mills were the main type of sawmill found in early New England and especially prominent in Maine with its many rivers and streams. These early mills used a reciprocating sash saw, which has a rigid, straight blade. Much like a jigsaw, a sash saw moves up and down, leaving straight saw marks on the wood. The first circular-saw mill came to Maine in 1860 on the Kenduskeag River. Thus, unless material was shipped in from another state, any lumber sawn circularly in Maine was sawn after this date. The braces in the barn at bents six, seven and eight display marks made by a circular saw.

The flattened, cutout areas called the housings were a decidedly new approach to working with the uneven nature of hewn material. Modern builders have it pretty easy today. Not only is our lumber straight and smooth, but it's also square and relatively uniform. This was mere fantasy to anyone working with hand-hewn material, which was nearly everyone in rural nineteenth-century Maine. Hand-hewn material not only varied in cross section but was also neither smooth nor square. It's impossible to cut all of a building's braces to a uniform length when the posts and beams they join vary in size. Each and every brace must be different. Thus early scribe-rule builders had to custom cut their braces. A new solution was to cut out housings to a predetermined, uniform depth in every post and beam where a brace would intersect.

At some point, a carpenter had a sort of epiphany, realizing that a perfect, slightly smaller beam exists within the timber itself. Material evidence and written records suggest this notion was conceived sometime in the early nineteenth century in New England. The concept goes something like this: The builder created flat housings in the timber to a predetermined depth at the points where the joints intersect, thereby rendering the distance between them, like the length of a brace, the same. One way this was done in the early 1800s was to snap a line down the center of a timber. If you had an eight- by eight-inch timber, for example, you might use seven inches as your housed-within "perfect timber." From the centerline, you would then measure three and a half inches toward the outside of the timber and cut your housing to this depth. The same would be done to the corresponding timber, resulting in a consistent, repeatable dimension. All of the braces could then be cut at once with a high degree of certainty that they would fit. This new method came to be known as "square-rule" and was first mentioned in Edward Shaw's *Civil Architecture* (1836).

In essence, the square-rule can be identified from its predecessor, the scribe-rule, by the presence of these housings, as well as the absence of any roman numerals (also called "marriage marks"). With the square-rule, few if any items had to be custom fitted and "scribed" in place, so there was no need to mark pieces that were to be paired together. The new method can then be said to be keeping with the phenomenon of interchangeable parts, which found its way into nearly every industry in the nineteenth century. The barn on Hio Ridge Road is a fine example of how these two methods can be found together. It all makes sense. Besides the saw marks and joinery alterations that speak to different eras of construction, an eighty-foot barn would have been far too large, indeed unusual, for a family operation out here in the far-off hinterlands of mid-1830s Maine.

In 1927, nearly one hundred years after the raising of this barn and home, Lois Ann Deering was born in an upstairs room in the attached house. She lived here until she was eighteen. Now in her mid-eighties, Mrs. Starbird lives in the Solon area and never realized the barn was added to. To her, it was always as is. Her father, Ralph Deering, scratched a living from the land, milked cows and sold apples until his death in 1946. Lois has some wonderful memories and is glad its current owners, David and Terri Gagnon (who purchased the property in 2010), plan on preserving the land and its beautiful barn.

Lois said the family always had cows. Her father Ralph was born here in 1893 and developed a herd of registered Guernseys.

"I can remember when we sold cream," Lois said. "There was a hand-crank cream separator in the milk room. The cream was taken to Hiram Creamery. The skim milk was clobbered (soured) and fed to pigs and hens. The family used whole milk. Sometimes we would save out a day's cream to make butter."

The farm sold milk, too. Before pasteurization regulations made it problematic, the Deerings sold raw milk to nearby Camp Winona on Moose Pond, a boys' camp that continues operations today. Electricity didn't come to the farm until around the time of the Rural Electrification Act of 1936, a mission that sought to supply the infrastructure and funding necessary to electrify isolated U.S. farms. The government appropriated

$50 million in the act's first year alone, indicating this was a substantial government expenditure in the years following the Great Depression.

"Dad, my grandparents and the two Evans families had to agree to pay certain amounts for five years," Lois recalls. "My dad agreed to $7.50 a month for five whole years of electric service. People didn't hesitate to tell him he was crazy. He got a milking machine then, with its very distinctive put-put-put sound. An electric milk cooler for the milk room was installed, which meant an end to the very arduous chore of cutting, hauling and storing ice in the winter."

Before modern electricity came to the farm, a crude gasoline-powered generator was used to meet some of the farm's needs. However, fuel was an expense and was much harder to come by in the 1930s and '40s. Indeed, most farmers relied on naturally harvested ice to preserve milk in the old days. Many farmers built shallow field ponds where ice could be collected for their commercial dairy products and for home use. The Deerings got their ice from nearby Moose Pond. In the old icehouse that was sheltered from the sun on the north side of the barn, a block and tackle was set up to make Ralph Deering's chores a little easier. With a pair of tongs attached, Ralph used the block and tackle to grab an ice cake. He then swung it into the nearby milk room and plunged it up and down in a tank of water to remove the sawdust that had insulated the ice.

Life was different in those days. Lois remembered her father milking the cows twice a day. Sometimes a hired man assisted in the milking schedule and had dinner with the family. With the advent of electricity came the milking machine and a new, larger and relocated milk room, complete with a refrigerated tank. One year, when Lois was about fourteen years old, she and her younger brother Mike were pressed into service in the barn after their father suffered an accident working in the woods.

"I took over the barn work twice," Lois recalled. "Once when dad got hurt and couldn't handle things for several days. [The] hired man, George, was available to help then. Next time was when my mother was ill. Mike was nine then, and we handled much it for over a week. George, long retired, helped out some. I had been working away and was not in shape for barn work. My forearms ached from hand-stripping the cows after removing the milking machines."

The barn is 34.5 feet wide, a little narrower than most barns, which typically measure 40 feet. It's almost exactly two rods wide (33 feet) but not quite. One observation gleaned from barn study is that old barns typically don't fall neatly on modern tape measures. Because later barn constructions

Even though it was built by a family of English descent, this barn does not have an English tying joint and jowled post configuration. It displays a connected-girt frame, an American design. Rather than a continuous top plate, frame sections (bents) are joined instead by horizontal dropped girts.

At eighty feet, this barn is about twice as long as it was when first built. Though wholly constructed of hand-hewn timber, subtle clues reveal it was not built all at once. Two distinctly different styles of joinery and dissimilar saw marks on both bracing and boarding are found within.

used stud layouts and plywood, today's buildings are typically multiples of 4 feet. But what drove the sizes of yesteryear's buildings? Such odd lengths leave us wondering what else barn builders were using as a basis of measurement.

The frame is made of seven bents that are irregularly spaced on thirteen- to fourteen-foot centers. The doorway and main aisle, which measure about eleven feet in width, are located in the center. Both sides of the aisle are flanked by twelve-foot sections. It seems the builder could have made the aisle twelve feet long as well, which would give the barn a thirty-six-foot dimension, but perhaps only the builders know why this was never done.

Cattle were kept to the right on the southernmost side. Rather than utilizing flared posts with an English tying joint and a continuous-top wall plate, the barn is built according to an arrangement that is sometimes referred to as a connected-girt system, so-called because wall posts are joined by segmented girts that are typically dropped eight inches to two feet from the posts' top. This system is distinctly American and is not typically found outside of New England. It is thought to be principally a northern New England phenomenon. When the barn was lengthened, its builder employed the exact same style of construction as the original section, except he used the square rule method.

Though devoid of animals today, there's still plenty of evidence of dairy cattle in the barn. The south section's interior is whitewashed, and the cattle tie-up remains. There is also an old 1961 listing of milking details called the "Eastern States Dairy Herd Record" that still hangs on a nail in the milk room; its presence indicates that dairy was a force here well after the Deering family left in the mid- to late 1940s.

CHAPTER TWO

THE OLD MAJESTICS

Big Haylofts and Fancy Cupolas

The time between the last decades of the nineteenth century and the early twentieth century is when big New England barns reached their zenith. This was the Victorian Age: The big, beautiful barns had arrived. Maine had continued its transformation from beef and sheep to dairy farming during this period, and ever-larger dairy barns with their fancy cupolas graced the land. These stately structures averaged 40 by 60 feet, though you can find some as large as 120 feet.

These "old majestics" were a departure from the plain and understated storehouses of earlier times and were a statement built by the prospering agriculturists of the day, almost all of whom had Republican values.

Around the same time our grand barns appeared, Maine's Republican Party also formed. In the mid-nineteenth century, Maine's Republican Party stood on a prohibition and abolitionist platform. The state's first Republican governor, Hannibal Hamlin, was born in Oxford County in 1809 and went on to become Abraham Lincoln's vice president. Initially a Democrat, Hamlin's sympathies with the antislavery effort caused him to switch parties. Maine was largely Republican for nearly one hundred years after Hamlin's rise and was among the six states to vote against Democrat Franklin Delano Roosevelt in the 1932 presidential election.

With gable roofs and big haylofts, roof trimmings on the old majestics are more ornate, having pronounced gables and soffit-area embellishments. Large cupolas with fancy vents and an architectural

An old majestic in Milo from 1880. These big, stately barns heralded a new era of prosperity, technology and the long march toward farming's commercialization.

style topped by bold weathervanes heralded a different expression to New England architecture at the time these barns were built. In fact, many other structures, such as homes, churches and public buildings, also saw a distinct architectural shift in the latter half of the Victorian period (1837–1901), which is considered to be the beginning of modern times. Main entryways that had been placed along the eaves wall were now being replaced with gable-entry designs. Also in this new era, technology allowed operations to become increasingly larger, and dairy emerged on the landscape in a big way. Farming in Maine reached its zenith around 1880. The point of commercialization had begun. Specialization in a certain commodity or crop was a basic economic survival strategy that Maine farmers could no longer ignore. Contrary to our idealistic notions and romantic feelings, most of Maine is not prime farmland. Our growing season is short and the soil rocky. The opening of the Erie Canal in 1825 began to tap the western New York and Pennsylvania regions and was ultimately followed by the railroads that further tapped the "bread basket" of the Midwest. With the advent of these two industrial innovations, the Maine farmer found himself struggling more and more against an unfavorable economic tide. It was time to rethink farming techniques.

Livestock in the form of dairy cattle became the saving grace and ultimately kept much of the Maine farming tradition alive well into the Great Depression. The first dairymen association was formed in the Pine Tree State in 1874, and dairying would soon become our leading industry; it gave us our grandest barns. An address by Professor L.C. Bateman of Lewiston to the Maine Dairyman's Association found in *Agriculture of Maine: Sixth Annual Report of the Commissioner of Agriculture of the State of Maine* (1907) summarizes the progress attained in both barns and dairying after the Civil War:

> *I am here this evening to say a word of welcome to you who represent the happy homes of Maine. You are also representatives of the great dairy interests of this State. Dairying is today simply in its infancy. I remember when a boy, and some of you older ones can easily remember, the old barn with its great cracks, the scrub cow, the old milking stool. But a wonderful change has come as the years have passed by. Today we find the blooded cow; today we find a better barn, a better house. We find the barn shingled or clapboarded and painted, and a neatly kept lawn around the buildings. Everything has been progressing and advancing with giant strides since you and I were boys, and I believe the future will see as great an advance in this industry.*

It was indeed a time of progress; the first glimmers of modernization were here. What made these newer barns so majestic was their sheer size and ornamentation. Decorative elements such as the rooftop cupolas were also downright functional. These big barns were loaded with hay, and as any farmer knows, an overly hot hayloft is a recipe for trouble. Hay is prone to spontaneous combustion, and damp hay exacerbates this. Some seasoned farmers tell of plunging their hands into a stack of loose hay years ago only to find it so hot that they could not hold it there.

We can look at one of these old majestics today and be completely ignorant to the fact that they actually became quite refined in terms of use and design. By the late nineteenth century, floor plans, hay storage and manure handling had become something of a science. Farming journals spoke of the advantages of ramps and cellars that allowed gravity to ease everyday farm chores.

Technological advancements in the lumber industry also ushered in the replacement of hand-hewn frames with structures made of sawn timber. With the end of the Civil War in 1864, transportation methods such as railroads made standardized lumber more readily available. As a result, most barns that were built after the Civil War were constructed with sawed timber. Pegged mortise and tenon joinery still ruled the day, but the field of carpentry was changing in the years after the war. Standardized timbers and lumber meant construction could be simplified. It was a time of transition, not only socially but technologically. The "joiner," the time-honored apprenticed carpenter of old, was about to be challenged.

A HIGH-DRIVE BANK BARN: NEW GLOUCESTER

Gravity made chores easier in a high-drive. There is one ramped barn in particular located on Woodman Road in New Gloucester. Dan Pierce grew up in town and returned to purchase this farmstead in the late 1990s.

The high-drive bank-barn design was developed during the mid-nineteenth century. An 1830 account in the farming journal *New England Farmer* attributes the development of an early high-drive to the Shaker community of Harvard, Massachusetts. The group was known for their ingenuity and resourcefulness, and the barn itself may well have been the first of its kind. A typical high-drive is built on a slope, has three or more floors and has a ramp at a gable end that allows hay to be hauled to the top floor, which is often just a center aisle. The hay can then be pitched down to the haymow(s) from above. In the 1830s, these ramps oftentimes were not made to exit out the other end of the barn, and the horses or oxen had to be turned around on a wider section at the other end.

Farmers were not averse to incorporating technology in their barns: Anything that made labor easier was readily adopted. Even if it was as simple as employing gravity through the use of ramps and basements, these barns had become refined, and their attributes were enthusiastically discussed in farming journals of the day. Once account from an 1867 edition of *New*

With a ramp and multiple floors, this old majestic in New Gloucester is what's known as a high-drive bank barn.

England Farmer recommends this design to a reader who wrote in for advice on barn construction:

> *Can you build your barn on a side hill, so as to drive in at the gable end, and have all your pitching* down *instead of up? The barn floor, in such case, would be high up, and all the stock below it. This is worth thinking of. If you have a suitable place, would it not be good economy to look at some barns constructed in that manner? The barn is a thing of every-day use for the farmer as long as he is farming, and it is, therefore, important that it be so constructed as to keep the stock and fodder safely, and save as much labor as possible.*

Pierce's barn is three stories high. According to documents from the New Gloucester Historical Society, this was the homestead of Nicholas Rideout, who was born in the neighboring town of Pownal in 1822. He came to settle on Woodman Road after marrying Charlotte Woodman. Their home was built in 1851. The barn was likely erected shortly after. According to documents, he "had no money, but something of more value, willing hands and resolution to carry whatever he undertook."

The barn Rideout built measures forty-two by seventy square feet It's big and has a hand-hewn frame of seven bents. But instead of being fashioned using the old scribe-rule method, it was built from reused timber via the square rule as demonstrated by the empty mortises in many of the beams. Sawn timber was also used in the barn's construction, suggesting something of a hybrid style. Sawn studs were installed between each bent in the horizontal boarding.

Boards in the stairwell have been signed *N.B. Rideout, 1884* in pencil. The roof is a common rafter system, but it is not the original framing. The wall plates over each main post have empty housings in them where the major rafters, which would have been used in a traditional purlin framing system, once sat. Based on the hybrid style, it appears Rideout's barn was built from limited means, as Rideout himself was restricted somewhat financially. By wedding Charlotte Woodman, whose family the road is named after, Rideout received good land to work, but he had yet to make a name for himself. His high-tech barn would no doubt contribute to his future prosperity.

Today, Pierce keeps sheep and chickens. Soon after he and his wife purchased this barn, they decided to give it some much-needed care. Pierce contacted a prominent building mover, Clayton Copp and Sons of Cumberland, who jacked up and suspended the entire barn on cribbing and steel I-beams in order to do some serious foundation work. Pierce said the looming restoration likely dissuaded a few potential buyers when the property was on the market. A thorough restoration of the sills and a basic releveling of the structure were needed.

Originally built on a base of split granite and stone, Pierce had a modern concrete foundation poured under three walls. He decided to retain the original wall section that faces the ramp. Replacing this would have disturbed the quaint attributes of the original ramp design. To allow access to the first floor, the ramp was constructed in two parts: a stone and earthen slope was set at the ground with a sixteen-foot, wooden bridge connecting to the second floor of the barn. An old sketch of the property shows a team of animals—most likely oxen—hauling in a wagon rounded high with loose hay. The drawing clearly shows a two-part ramp with an opening to the first floor beneath, indicating that this was the barn's original design. The wooden ramp section, though likely a replacement, was built of stout timbers. Three

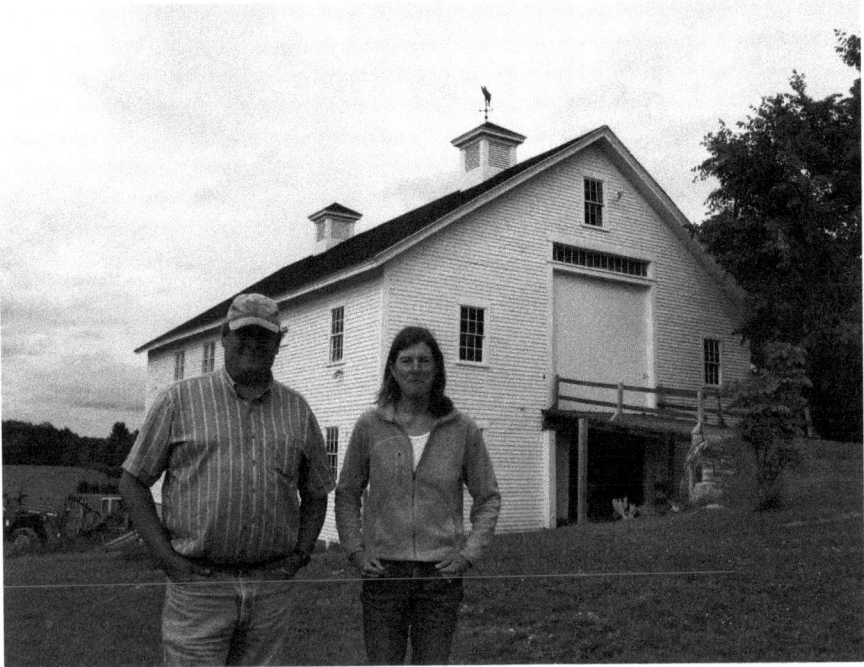

Dan and Sarah Pierce saved this barn from further decline by having a new foundation put under it.

eight- by sixteen-inch beams (possibly claimed from a railroad bridge) carry the load.

Instead of a full top floor, most high-drive bank barns have an aisle on the top story coming off the ramp, while the first floor is open on one or more sides to the peak. This allows hay to be efficiently pitched down from the aisle above. Today, the top floor of Pierce's barn is completely boarded over and has been converted for more modern uses, such as a woodworking shop. This barn doesn't have just one cupola but two, both of which help ventilate the loft. They also work to evacuate the manure basement. Wooden chutes built into the roof and wall framing siphon out the humid cellar space. Pierce likes to woodwork, and he rebuilt these cupolas himself. Measuring almost five by five square feet, they're bigger than they look from the ground. Pierce had to have a crane position them at the peak. With the two cupolas sitting in good proportion atop the roof, this barn is a stately structure best viewed from Route 231 after the foliage has dropped.

A prospering agriculturalist that commissioned a grand barn, Nicholas Rideout was well known and praised in nineteenth-century agricultural circles in Cumberland County. *Courtesy of the New Gloucester Historical Society.*

The technological innovations of the barn indicate that Nicholas Rideout became a prospering agriculturalist. This high-drive barn made for an efficient operation in its day. The hay came in up top, while the manure was stored under cover below. The cattle resided in the middle. A document provided by the New Gloucester Historical Society summed up Rideout's reputation:

> *In politics Mr. Rideout is a Republican, and is a member of the Congregational Church of New Gloucester. He is interested in and a promoter of good society, and of all enterprises of a charitable nature. He is a thrifty, enterprising farmer, and among the best agriculturalists of Cumberland County.*

ONE HUNDRED FEET IN HIRAM

A mammoth Old Majestic on Tripptown Road in Hiram is a brilliant example of how our barns increased in size following the Civil War. It's a stand-alone barn and is located just across the road from its original farmhouse. It measures one hundred feet long and forty-one feet wide.

Built around a hand-hewn frame, this old majestic is one hundred feet long. Early owners raised dairy cattle. Its current owners do not own livestock, but they do sell hay and keep scores of square bales inside.

The first family to own this parcel was none other than the Wadsworth family, ancestors of the celebrated poet Henry Wadsworth Longfellow (1807–1882). For his Revolutionary War service, the poet's grandfather, General Peleg Wadsworth, acquired 7,800 acres of land in what would later become the town of Hiram. Before Maine became a state, Peleg Wadsworth was a senator and represented the District of Maine in the Massachusetts Legislature. The general became the founder of Hiram, which was originally part of York County. Over residents' objections in 1805, Hiram reluctantly joined the then newly formed Oxford County, and it remains under that county's jurisdiction today.

It's thought that Peleg Thompson Wadsworth (1845–1915), the general's great-grandson, built the barn, and construction details support this. For one, the building's size is immense. The barn was constructed in one act and was not added to later. It's unlikely a barn of this stature would have been found on a private Maine farm in the early 1800s. Only large communities

A connected-girt frame. Instead of raising two one-hundred-foot-long walls, each bent is joined in segments via connecting girts. Note the tie beam on the left that sticks out beyond the wall post and supports the roof rafter while also providing the building with an overhang.

like the Shakers, or perhaps state-run facilities in pre–Civil War days, typically built barns of this scale. Most barns back then were half this length. Another indicator that it was constructed in the late nineteenth century is the absence of jowled posts and English tying joints. The bore marks on the split granite foundation indicate the barn was built after 1830, while the presence of an embellished roof trim and a cupola and the existence of square-rule joinery are all signs that suggest it was built sometime in the latter nineteenth-century.

This is a well-built barn with a nine-bent, connected-girt frame and a mixture of hewn and sawn timber. All major timbers are hand-hewn, while shorter members, including the connecting girts, are sawn.

In 2010, Sally Williams of the Hiram Historical Society set out to document every barn in the town of Hiram, compiling the better examples into a popular calendar that raised funds for the society. This old majestic graced the month of May and is rightfully labeled as a "side-bank" barn since it is on a slope that ran perpendicular to its length, a feature that naturally provides access to a manure basement below.

The barn was built during the apex of farming in Maine. Accounts state that Peleg Thompson Wadsworth was an able agriculturist and a Republican and also ran a dairy where he raised excellent stock. He inherited this property from the family line and built up a fine enterprise. Some old dairy indicators remain in the barn, and dairying may have continued after the Wadsworth family sold this farm. There's whitewashing along the south facing side directly over the manure basement. An interior square silo is located in the middle on the opposite side. According to Clarence Day's *Farming in Maine, 1860–1940* (1963), the state's barns received their first silos right around the time this barn was built. The early silos were square and located inside the building. Early on, silos were only found on the more prominent farming operations. Perhaps Wadsworth was an early pioneer in this new silo phenomenon in the region.

Many farmers were unaccustomed to the new kind of feed held within, known as ensilage, which was comprised primarily of corn. A section in the 1892 publication *Agriculture of Maine: Annual Report to the Secretary* reads as minutes from a meeting where a professor of agriculture answers questions from a number of dairymen:

> *Ques: Is ensilage as good as English hay?*
> *Ans: Good judges think that one and one-half to three tons its worth as much as a ton of good English hay.*

The same report answered how to build a square, interior silo:

> *Ques: What is the best method of building the silo?*
> *Ans: What I consider the best is made of two by ten, set up edgewise and covered on the inside with two thicknesses of boards, with building paper between, with gas tar slightly thinned with gasoline, so it is put on with a brush; the inner lining is painted with that before the building paper is put on; then the inside of the silo is painted after the silo is all made, the outside being just the thickness of the sheathing. The two by ten, sixteen inches apart, gives strength enough.*

These instructions meant there was a six-inch space between each horizontal two- by ten-inch board. In time, farmers discovered that this and other square designs were not strong enough to hold tons of feed, which was purposely packed and weighted down, sometimes with planks and rocks at the top, to prevent the natural action of heat from building within. Reportedly, the tighter a silo was built and packed—preventing an exchange of air—the less apt it was to generate heat. This is certainly why it was recommend to add a layer of building paper between the layers of boarding. Some silos were finished inside with plaster and lath, which not only sealed its contents but also frustrated any rodents who sought access. Most farmers kept a few barn cats around for a good reason.

In time, after the failures of many of these square designs, the round silo, which was surrounded by hoops of metal rods, became popular. A good analogy comparing the two designs can be seen in a paper cup. There's a reason why paper cups are round. They're simply much stronger this way. Imagine a square paper cup. It would be inferior in comparison because it could not only resist pressure from the grasp of your hand, it's ability to hold the force of any liquid would also be greatly reduced.

These days, the barn is owned by brothers Gene and George Staccy who've owned it since 1986. The Staceys do not keep livestock but use the barn to store and sell hay they cut from the land. Other families that have claimed ownership over the years include the Dexters and the Blanchards.

A MILO MAJESTIC

One of the most majestic barns left in the state can be found on Route 11 in the town of Milo. The barn is at the Katahdin Country Club. Milo, located just east of Dover-Foxcroft on Route 16, has a history intimately linked with Maine's railroads. A railcar building and repair shop for the Bangor and Aroostook, once the second-largest shop in New England, operated in town for many years. The shops still function in a scaled-down version under the ownership of The Montreal, Maine & Atlantic. Many sawmills were located in Milo, too. Wooden spools by the millions were made by the American Thread Company (1902–1975), one of the country's last manufactures of wooden spools. Shoemaking was also a large industry here. Dexter Shoe Company operated here from 1966 to 2000.

Probably the most notable feature about the barn at Katahdin Country Club is its slate roof, cupola and gable ends. Slate roofs are a common feature of Milo buildings because of the town's proximity to slate quarries in nearby Brownville and Monson.

The date "1880" is nailed on the front of this barn. Before it became a golf course in the 1930s, this land was a potato field. The barn, however, looks a bit more prominent than its history suggests. Owned by the Gerrish family since 1940, much of its early detail and usage has been lost to the passage of time, but certain features suggest that it and the land likely belonged to a prominent individual. One can imagine a nice collection of buggies, sleighs and the required horses housed within; hay was likely piled high to the peak.

At forty by fifty square feet, the main barn has two lean-to additions along each eaves wall. There is no basement; the surrounding terrain is as flat as a football field.

You can't judge a book by its cover, and this is certainly true for barns. Like many passing by, you might suppose a slate roof such as this would require a serious supporting network of timber. Not so. This barn is

Covered in slate, this old majestic in Milo is protected from the elements by one of the most durable roofing materials ever put into practice. Slate quarrying was a large industry in this part of the state years ago.

A ship's knee within a hybrid frame of studs and timber. Circular-sawn standardized lumber began appearing in barns in the late nineteenth century.

made up of just four widely spaced bents that are about sixteen feet apart and are framed out of slim, circular-sawn six- by six-inch timbers. The roof is a common rafter system of closely spaced two- by six-inch lumber clad with horizontal boarding. The building is quite peculiar; there's hardly any bracing. Yet the bracing that is here is in the form of ship's knees, which can be found at each main post. Ship's knees are an element typically found in better-built barns. Between each post supporting each common rafter is a more contemporary network of closely spaced two- by six-inch studding.

If you study barns to any degree, you'll discover that those built around 1900 are really a hybrid of traditional heavy-timber and stud-frame styles. It's as if the builders were unsure of the era they were in. Before the Civil War, and a few years after, most barns were traditionally built of stout eight-by eight-inch hand-hewn timbers

As sawmills became prevalent and railroads allowed easier shipment of standardized lumber and timber, barns were built with smaller, circular-sawn posts and beams that might measure seven by seven inches. By the turn of the century, frames used even slimmer six- by six-inch timbers. Indeed, with the emergence of planks and common "two-by" lumber, heavy timber would soon disappear entirely. Nails and planks were much quicker and easier to fashion walls and roofs with. No apprenticed joiner was required. The system was also considerably lighter and thus much easier to raise. But these frames did not stand the test of time as well as their hewn forbearers. Currently, hundreds of rudimentary connections are in place only until the nails rust through.

That said, this barn is an absolute beauty to look at. The cupola is nicely set at a 45-degree angle. A beautiful arched window, something that would be equally at home in a church, graces the front gable end. All of this is covered in elegant slate work.

Slate is perhaps one of the best roofing materials ever devised. It's durable, beautiful and also fireproof—an important consideration in early villages when roofs were typically comprised of wood shingles. Many cities and towns have since banned wood-shingled roofs for this very reason. Embers blowing from one burning home could easily land and start a fire on another's roof. Because of the expense and specialized labor these days, slate is typically only found on high-end work. The slate roofer typically employs copper nails since the slate will outlast normal roofing nails.

Just how much weight is on this barn's roof? According to *The Carpenter's Cyclopedia* (1913), roofing slate typically came in thicknesses of $3/16$ and $5/16$ of an inch. Depending upon exposure (overlap), slate roofs could weigh as much as six pounds per square foot, making it one of the heaviest roofing materials available as it weighed only slightly less than lead roofing. Based on this, we can estimate the Katahdin Country Club barn's roof to weigh in at about seven tons. And that's just the roof surface, ignoring the two gable ends and large cupola that are also shielded in slate. In all likelihood, the walls of this barn are supporting some ten tons of roof weight, more if the necessary lumber and boarding are taken into consideration. And that's without any snow or wind loads. Interestingly, a slate roof at six pounds per square foot exerts the same force as a continuous forty-mile-an-hour wind. As lightly framed as this barn is, it's a testament that it's been able to withstand Maine weather for over a century. It looks like it will stand for many more years to come. No doubt, the lean-tos along each side (also roofed in slate) also act as stabilizing agents. Like bookends, these have likely assisted the structure over the years.

It is a beautiful building, and it's great to see a barn like this in the hands of owners who have faithfully maintained it.

AN OLD MAJESTIC ETCHED IN STONE: NEW GLOUCESTER

Not far from New Gloucester's town line, just off Route 100, sits another old majestic. At first glance, this barn looks like it might be older than its 1911 construction date. But its poured concrete foundation, nailed braces, fancy cupola and split-paned windows attest to a later period.

Originally built for horses and cattle, the barn was originally erected on two berms of earth with an open area in between. This was reportedly done to save the builders from excavating out a cellar space on the site, which is only slightly sloped. However, factors related to this undermined the barn's structural integrity over the years, and its current owner is in the process of remedying it with the help of his nephew.

Though it may be sagging and absent of paint, this barn and its surrounding acreage enrich the landscape just the same. What a subject to photograph or paint! The countless commuters who drive by the busy Route 100 and see this great barn change with the seasons no doubt find it enhances an otherwise mediocre stretch of road. If nothing else, this barn stands as a proud symbol of Maine's rural heritage.

Carmel Morin is the third generation on this particular property. The Witham family, his mother's family, has roots in town going back much further, back to the mid-1800s. Fire was a common occurrence that displaced folks in the nineteenth century, and the Morins came to this spot to start anew after a house fire around 1906. It would be a few years before this big detached barn was built. Originally, there was a separate and smaller barn beside the big forty-three- by sixty-eight-footer that stands today.

The farm has seen many uses over its history, including housing chickens, cattle, horses, rabbits and pigs and growing beans. Milk was produced here. Morin said a small milk house attached to the barn had to be moved farther away with the encroaching dairy regulations in the years before bulk tanks.

Morin, now a retired teacher, grew up on this property. In the year 2000, Morin and his siblings inherited it from their parents. Morin is not a full-

Carmel Morin and Ryan Tripp of New Gloucester aren't letting this old majestic succumb to the ravages of time.

Rather than using hand-hewn timber to build this barn, circular-sawn material was the way to go in the early twentieth century. Nails replaced the time-honored fashion of pegs in this joint. A nut at the end of a long threaded rod (an original detail) helps tie the frame together and is visible on the left side of this post.

time farmer but has raised the occasional beef cow. He keeps a few chickens and wants desperately to save the barn from further deterioration, most of which has been caused by water damage. Building on berms of earth may have saved the task of excavating a cellar area, but it allowed water to pool and flow underneath. Subsequent freezing and thawing has undermined the poured foundation at each gable end, as well as the post footings at its center.

A barn of this size can be an immense challenge to maintain. A few years ago Morin and his nephew jacked up the barn and put in temporary supports to mitigate the sagging. But the natural flow of water beneath the barn worked against them. Long-standing drainage issues forced them to bring in an excavator and reconfigure some of the landscape.

On close inspection, the 1911 construction date reveals some modern approaches to barn building. It was the twentieth century after all, and there's a sense that those who built the barn were somewhat unsure of the era they were in. In truth, they were very much between two ages of time.

Details of this barn include a hybrid frame of six bents made of circular-sawn timber with sawn studs and common rafters in between. Instead of being mortised and pegged in place, the bracing was nailed. Many principal joints were pegged, but a combination of bolting and nailing can be seen at some of the prominent joint intersections, a detail not typically seen before 1900.

The bolts display older square-shaped nuts, and the timbers are slightly smaller than expected for an earlier frame, measuring seven by seven inches. (Wide boarding was still available in 1911.) Covering the walls are full one-inch thick boards with circular saw marks. Many of these boards measure sixteen inches across.

The building is still packed with items from the farm's past. There is an old steel-wheeled cart and various horse tack on the walls. As a child, along with his siblings, Morin plucked chickens his father had dispatched in the barn. It was a small family farm, and as was typical to early days of barns with their origins as civic buildings, this barn held hay for the surrounding community. After World War II, a neighbor in the area stored hay here

Farming and the buildings associated with it defined the identity of this family, so much so that the children chose to have the image of the family barn emblazoned on this headstone when the parents died. The stone can be found in a New Gloucester cemetery.

and paid the insurance as a trade-off, proving a little bartering could still be found in these communities. The barn stands today as an old majestic, an icon of a once proud past. It was important enough to the Morin family that when their father, Raymond passed in 1998 (he was born in 1911, the very year the barn was constructed) and again when their mother Ruth passed in 2000, an image of the barn was emblazoned with a laser-etching process upon the family headstone. The stone can be found at the New Gloucester Cemetery across from the fairgrounds in what's known as the Upper Village.

LONG TIE BEAMS AT GRASSLAND FARM: SKOWHEGAN

It happened on an unsuspecting afternoon. Garin Smith decided to fetch a tool from the ground floor of his barn and saw flames running along some wiring. A large hay-drying fan that was in use on the floor above had grounded out, causing a fire to break out along the circuit. Luckily, Smith's quick actions saved the big white barn at Grassland Farm before any serious damage brought an untimely end to its long history.

Garin and Sarah Smith run an organic dairy operation here in Skowhegan. Both say they would rather see the house burn than the barn—that is, as long as everyone got out safely. That way they could continue making money while worrying about rebuilding their home. If the barn burns, their ability to earn a living goes up in smoke, too.

The Smiths purchased this place from Sarah's father, Robie, in 2007, after he had milked cows for twenty years. Garin and Sarah chose to operate an organic dairy. Some forty to fifty calves are born here each year.

"I wouldn't do it any other way," Garin said on choosing to go organic. "I'm not at the whim of a drug salesman pressuring me that this is the only way to operate. Organic farmers can keep to themselves a little more and make decisions based on the livelihood of the animals."

The first thing you notice about this barn is its sheer size. It measures 42 by 106 feet. With 18-foot posts, it is one of the taller barns around. Post height changed as barns evolved through the years here in Maine. Older barns typically have shorter posts, while newer ones are frequently higher. Hay storage and commercial-scale farming requirements drove these decisions.

Garin and Sarah Smith are a young family raising more than just livestock and vegetables on this Skowhegan farm.

It's worth noting some particular details on the barn's construction. First, the tie beams in this building are continuous forty-two-foot-long eight- by eight-inch timbers—no small task, considering most sawmills have trouble producing anything longer than twenty-four feet. The timbers are circular-sawn, which helps pinpoint the structure's age. As aforementioned, the first circular sawmills in Maine appeared around 1860. Earlier versions had been in use, but these only produced clapboards, shingles and other small stock. Lumber and timber produced by the circular saw came later.

In volume two of *History of the Lumber Industry in America* (1907), James Elliott Defebaugh writes:

> *The first circular saw ever started in Maine was taken there by George Page, of Baltimore, and put into the waterpower mill of John Webster, on the Kenduskeag Stream. The saw was forty-eight inches in diameter and was made by Gage, Hubbard & Co…The permanent introduction*

of rotary saws came in about 1860, although only a few were in use for years thereafter.

The trees necessary to yield the barn's tie beams must have been significant logs. To yield an eight- by eight-inch timber, a log must be almost a foot in diameter (11 $^5/_{16}$ inches) over its entire required length. And that's assuming it's reasonably straight.

The big barn wasn't always so long; an addition came in the 1970s. Constructed in a similar fashion, the addition put on three more bents (about forty extra feet of length). The tie beams on these bents are not continuous but are spliced and bolted together in the center of the barn. Upon inspecting this detail, an interesting feature is noticeable. With nine bents overall, the sixth bent from the front is where something curious occurred. The rear wall of the barn used to be here, but instead of stripping the boards off the frame and adding on to the barn, whoever built the addition decided to move the entire back wall, sheathing, windows and all to its final position at the rear of the newly-configured barn. As such, a discriminating eye will notice the last bent has a continuous tie beam, just like the original section. The tie beams are important structural members in this barn. They stop the walls from spreading under a roof load that wants to continuously push the walls outward. That's a considerable force given the size of this roof. Add a wind load (Garin Smith said the area gets whipping in winter) and the magnitude increases.

Continuous timber is important to a frame's integrity. Despite the increase and ease of obtaining sawn timber after the Civil War, some barn builders continued to fashion their own hand-hewn stock for the longest and most important pieces, such as tie beams and wall plates. This can explain the miscellany of stock types in a barn frame. You simply can't beat nature's own design: the unbroken strength of continuous timber is hard to improve upon.

For a barnologist, it would be nice to know the barn that could claim the title of "longest timber" in Maine. Although not a barn, the 1807 Portland Observatory on Munjoy Hill is very likely in the top ten. The eight-sided structure sports eight continuous sixty-five-foot posts, which were contracted, cut and roughly squared in the town of Windham for the sum of twelve dollars each. Raising this structure must have been a sight to see.

Raising the big white barn on Grassland Farm would have been a grand task, too. Though its early history is murky and buried in the vaults of time, William Bradbury, who arrived here in the 1850s, likely raised the barn. He did not build the barn when he arrived, since the aforementioned construction details point to a later date. Many elements here suggest late nineteenth to early twentieth century. For instance, cattle was held down below in the basement, not on the second floor as would have been the case in the nineteenth century. Additionally, the foundation is poured concrete, though it's possible this was done at a later time. However, what classifies the barn as a nineteenth-century construction is the vertical wall boarding in the original section. The fact that prominent joints are pegged also indicates it is from the nineteenth century. Horizontal roof sheathing is found over a common rafter frame.

Besides owning this farm on the banks of the Wesserunsett Stream, William Bradbury was part owner of nearby Malbon's Mills, which got its start way back in 1790. The locals say this mill sawed the timber for Bradbury's barn, and being part owner of the mill, he was probably able to acquire continuous forty-two-foot timber easier then the next guy could have.

This is a prominent barn with a history of prominent people; it was the first barn in the area to get electricity. After Bradbury left about 1920, Blin Page, who later ran unsuccessfully for governor as a Republican in 1936, bought this as a hobby farm. Page spouted the campaign slogan, "Turn to Page 1936." He built a two-story ell on the barn with a beautifully paneled tongue and groove office upstairs and made a living off churning butter in a north room that was added to the house.

CHAPTER THREE

OUR BARNS

Assorted Barns, Assorted People

Our Barns: Talking with the "Barn Generation": Oxford

BY DON PERKINS

Note: This article first appeared in the Advertiser Democrat *on April 21, 2011, as part of a series on local barns and their associated people.*

Oxford—Last Saturday was an interesting day. With the prospects of one barn I'd planned to feature for this series falling through, I was in dire need of a "plan B." Thus, I headed North up Route 26 searching for another barn to explore with no idea where I might end up or who I might meet.

I soon spied a handsome looking small white barn at the corner of Route 26 and Station Road.

"Ah, an English barn," I thought. "That's interesting; I haven't written about too many of these." It was built on a slope, and I spied what looked like an old manure basement. Although it appeared this barn had been finished off inside and perhaps had other uses now, I still thought it was a nice prospect. I parked the car and proceeded toward the front door.

"Come on in, come on in!" a friendly old gentleman said almost immediately as he fumbled with the doorknob and gestured me inside. I was surprised how welcoming Bob Bartlett was. Most of the time when encountered with a stranger, folks will hang in the doorway and give me a good look-over, at which point I typically present my card and explain I'm interested in their barn.

Mr. Bartlett didn't really seem to care why I'd come. He promptly offered me a seat in his living room and we began to chat.

"I write a series about barns for the *Advertiser Democrat* in Norway," I explained, handing him my card.

"Barns," he said as he gave both me and the card a closer examination.

"I noticed you have a small English barn here," I asked. "Can I take a look at it?"

"What, that thing?" he said with indifference. "That's not old, at least not what I would call old. It's sawn timber, maybe 1900. I'll show it to you in a minute."

With that, I began thinking I should move on, that my earlier suspicions were right. This wasn't really an old barn at all. However, Bob Bartlett showed no signs of letting me off that easy. As he sat in his easy chair, he packed his pipe and struck a match to a fresh quantity of Captain Black. His dog rested comfortably on the couch.

"How long have you lived here?" I asked, trying to feel things out.

"Oh, about twenty years," he said, getting his pipe burning to his liking. "I grew up in Montville, near Belfast. I was the town manager for Norway."

I spied some woodworking magazines on his coffee table and noticed a beautiful old bookcase with glass doors along the far wall. It was tall, probably seven feet high with nice ornamentation at the top. As a former woodworker, I thought this was a potential point of commonality that might break the ice for us. I illuminated my woodworking background and asked what kind of wood the case was and if I might take a closer look.

"Sure," he said. "Help yourself."

What looked like cherry from across the room turned out to be something different; I wasn't quite sure what it was, perhaps mahogany. I did notice some nicely contrasting maple burl accents. Bob guessed it was walnut, but I could tell he wasn't quite sure either.

It was when I looked closer that I saw the old books inside. My interest was instantly piqued at seeing such titles as *Keeping Livestock Healthy* (1942), *The Principles of Dairying* and *Animal Sanitation and Disease Control*. And there were others. I just knew there had to be some solid information on barn history within these pages—like how disease factors changed elements in our barns. Getting a date range on some of these modifications and the

Our Barns

Robert Bartlett enjoys his pipe in the early 1980s. The author enjoyed an impromptu chat on barns with Mr. Bartlett that proved quite fruitful. The exchange was the subject of a local newspaper article and part of a weekly series on barns in the Oxford Hills area. *Courtesy of the Bartlett family.*

subsequent regulations is notoriously difficult—areas of great interest to researchers like me.

"I used to be a tester for the Waldo County Dairy Heard Improvement Association," Bob explained, as I inquired about the books. "I used to test milk for butter-fat content."

I tried probing him again on the barn and whether or not I could take a look.

"We'll go in a minute," he said, taking another draw on his pipe. "I don't move too fast."

I sat back down and we started talking barns. I told him where I lived. He asked if I was or had ever been a farmer. I said no. He then asked me about rooftop cupolas and whether I knew what they were used for. He was testing me, probing someone half his age on an area of interest usually known by older, more seasoned folks.

"They're for ventilating the buildings," I answered. "They started appearing around 1850 or '60 and got pretty fancy in the late Victorian age."

Bob nodded in agreement.

I explained how keeping manure in a manure basement became all the rage among farmers in the early to mid-nineteenth century and that air quality in these barns eventually became problematic, especially in the winter when animals spend little if any time outdoors.

"The moisture from the manure combined with the breath of the animals would rise and condense on the underside of the cold roof boards," I explained. "This also made the hay unpalatable to the animals. But cupolas served a purpose in summer, too," I continued, "because you wanted to keep your hay cool."

Bob concurred and broke in. "Putting in green hay would give you problems," he said, referring to the composting action of moist hay. As any seasoned farmer knows, these conditions created immense heat within a mound of loose hay and could start a fire through spontaneous combustion. Indeed, many barns burned this way.

Wanting to gain additional credence with Bob, I remarked how a farmer I knew told me a common practice was to put salt down between layers of questionably dry hay, as it would draw the moisture out.

"Yes," Bob agreed with a nod. "The animals probably liked the taste as well."

We were beginning to hit it off nicely, and I sensed he enjoyed talking with someone about farming and barns. Soon enough, we ventured through the kitchen to the barn I had been inquiring about.

It was quickly apparent that this building had never had any animals housed within. Instead, previous owners had made a fine looking twenty-four- by thirty-four-foot garage with all the elements of a barn: a paved ramp [that lead] up to a nice sliding door, with old granite block and stone that had been mortared in nicely, giving it the appearance of an old barn foundation. And its multilevels, roof pitch and proportions gave it the hallmarks of a small barn. But this is just Bob's garage and woodworking shop. Details of its construction, including rough-cut dimensional lumber fixed with modern hardware such as joist hangers, suggest this building is fifty years old at best.

It was getting cold, so we came back in and sat some more. I was eager to hear about Bob's days as a dairy tester and his memories of barns, but I didn't want to overstay my welcome. One question in particular stood out.

"Ever seen a barn burn?" I asked.

"1941. I saw a barn burn, yes," he said. "My father woke me up at two o'clock in the morning [and] said [that] the barn [was] on fire. I got up and looked out the window. The barn was all ablaze, eighty-six feet long. We don't know what started it...[That was] October 20, 1941."

Bob was about ten years old at the time, and because the house was connected to the barn, everything burned flat. Their livestock was lost. Bad wiring was ruled out. Even though the Rural Electrification Act of 1936 provided low-cost loans to many, the Bartletts didn't have power because they simply couldn't afford it. After the fire, Bob said his father decided it was cheaper to relocate the family than to rebuild.

As we talked, we concurred that farms and barns are disappearing. Knowledge about barns is fleeting too. Bob said it's too bad, but many young people have romantic visions of farming. "They don't realize how much work is involved," he said. "You can't take a vacation."

I was fortunate to happen upon Bob Bartlett and engage him in conversation, and he was kind enough to lend me some of his old books. Perhaps some of the information contained within will grace these pages in the coming weeks and months. A big thank-you goes out to Mr. Bartlett, who is part of a generation that's a veritable storehouse of the common barn life and its fading memories.

Sadly, Bob Bartlett left us before this book went to print. He passed just before Christmas, on December 23, 2011.

POETRY AND MEMORIES: SEARSPORT

An English barn that is no longer English sits along Route 1 in Searsport, a major seaport whose seafaring tradition continues today. For the past forty years, this has been the on-and-off residence of Randy and Liz Dominic. The house is quite historic and is thought to have originally come from town founder David Sears' compound on Sears Island. According to Liz Dominic, the house was moved from the island to its current location by oxen, hauled over the ice when Penobscot Bay was frozen. An exact date is unknown, but the move likely took place in the early nineteenth century. The town was named after David Sears and was incorporated in 1845. Colonial settlements date back to the 1760s.

The reason this barn is described as no longer being an English one is because it has had some alterations done to it. Where there were once front and rear eaves entry doors is still apparent. Two fourteen-light transom windows look out of place without a door below them today, but they were likely kept to help light the barn's naturally dim interior. Today, the

Elizabeth Dominic at her antique store in a barn on Route 1 in Searsport. Dominic has fond memories of barns throughout her life and would like to see them preserved and celebrated.

barn is detached from the house, but it was once joined. Dominic has old photographs showing this.

Dominic loves barns and has operated an antique store called Primrose Farm Antiques from this outbuilding for many years. She and her husband lived in Massachusetts before deciding to move, and they purchased this property sight unseen.

"In those days, Route 1 was very busy when we first purchased this place," she said. "I told my husband that if I was ever going to have a shop that this is where I should have it."

The barn needed a little care and maintenance in order to get it ready for antique customers. It still had an old wood-shingled roof, and rain easily found its way in. "Before we did anything with the house, my husband said, 'If we're to save that barn we've got to cover that roof.'" A metal roof was soon installed.

The barn is a bit of a conundrum in its construction, which makes it difficult to date. Measuring 36.5 by 42.5 feet, it has a hand-hewn frame that consists of different joinery styles. All four corner posts are jowled, or flared, yet the middle posts flanking the old eaves entry doorway are not. These posts, as well as the jowled ones, have dropped tie beams that were mortised into them and wedged in place, suggesting a half-dovetailed tie beam tenon. The only way to insert a dovetailed tenon in a manner it will not withdraw is to cut an oversized mortise, insert the tenon and then wedge the top of it in place so it cannot rise up and pull out. Among other pieces in the frame, these tie beams have empty mortises in them at odd locations, suggesting the building was constructed of salvaged timber, which was actually a very common practice years ago (evidence of this is found all over Maine). Hewing logs into beams was laborious and time-consuming. If one could find sound timbers that had already been squared, whether they were from an abandoned building or gleaned from a partial fire or other wreck, it made sense to reuse the material.

All the braces in the building are hand-hewn, which can suggest a building to be quite old, but a few factors must be taken into account in dating the barn. The barn's remote location and the economic wherewithal of the builder are starters. In some localities, hewn bracing may indicate that the building predates an area's first sawmill; thus all pieces of the frame had to be hewn onsite. Most hand-hewn barn frames exhibit sawn bracing. Along with boarding, the builder would have usually picked up a wagonload of small stock from the sawmill to use for bracing, wall girts and perhaps doorframes. However, the frame made of reused material suggests resources were likely scarce and that the farmer probably chose to save money by fashioning his own bracing and other secondary members.

The building is clad in wide, sash-sawn boarding from a water-powered mill, which is typically an indicator that the building was built before the Civil War. Wall boarding is applied vertically, whereas horizontal roof boards are attached over a common rafter roof system. The barn was probably sided later in its life; vertical wall boards naturally shed water.

Liz Dominic loves barns, and the one here in Searsport is not the first she's marveled at. Liz grew up in Gorham on a six-hundred-acre hay farm with a big barn. In the summer, the family would stay at a cottage outside of Bangor in Hermon. There were farm families all around in those parts, and Liz recalled playing with friends in one of the area's big barns.

"Farms and barns just became part of my life," she said. "I think that's why I feel the way I do about them. To me, a barn is the closest thing we have to European cathedrals, but they're made out of wood."

Now in her eighties, she recalled visiting her father's farm and barn in Gorham, which is still standing. Her father purchased the property, the main crop of which was hay, because of its proximity to Portland. "Everything was horse-drawn," she said. "There were big stables. There were no automobiles."

However, in the 1920s, only a few years after he first purchased the property, automobiles started taking over. "The gasoline engine became very popular," said Liz. "His customers switched."

When Liz was only about three years old, her father was forced to sell and took a job with a phone company. The family then moved to Massachusetts. Liz said the family visited Maine every summer. Like many of us, memories from childhood can easily be triggered decades later by a particular sight, sound or smell. For Liz, it was revisiting her father's old Gorham hay barn. Today, only two of the original six hundred acres remain with the barn. The rest has been developed into housing.

"It's kind of sad for me," Liz said. "He had a pond and used to cut ice for the winter. He did everything."

The last time Liz visited, she hadn't planned on going into the barn. She simply stopped the car out front and got out and looked.

"This young woman came out and asked if she could help," Liz said. "I said, 'I don't want to bother you, but this used to be my father's farm. It's a nostalgic thing for me.' The owner then asked me if I'd like to come into the barn. When I walked into the barn the smell of hay and animals must have hit some memory nerve because my eyes watered up. I almost cried in front of her. I was very surprised and a little embarrassed that that feeling came over me. I didn't actually remember the barn, but my body remembered it. Isn't that strange?"

Our Barns

Today, in Liz's antique shop, an old carpenter's adze hangs on the wall. The tag reads forty-five dollars. A similar item that was listed in the 1897 Sears Roebuck & Co. catalog is priced at ninety cents. The thirty-four-inch handles made out of second growth hickory are sold separately and are priced at forty cents.

Liz writes poetry from time to time. This one about barns was part of an exhibit at the Searsport Public Library years ago:

SANCTUARY
By ELIZABETH DOMINIC

I push my way
Into the vaulted coolness
Of the barn.
Summer Sun is left outside
To scorch and burn.
My ears will know
Those things I can not see—
The rhythmic crunch
Of horse's noon-time fare.
The rustle of a mouse
Upon the hay loft stair.
I hear the mighty bull snort air,
So restless to be free!
My heart is tethered just as he.
My eyes can see in dim light now.
I watch the swallows
Swoop and soar on high,
Busy families.
Here comes "Old Rex"
To rest inside with me.
He nuzzles in
To lie beside the door
And cocks an ear to hear alarm.
But all is calm and still
At noontime on the farm.
In this cathedral-kind of space
Is such a quiet place.

SHIP'S KNEES SPEAK OF COASTAL CONNECTIONS: HARPSWELL

The coastal town of Harpswell, which borders Brunswick, on Casco Bay in Cumberland County has some very intriguing barns. Several nice examples can be found on one of the town's highest points along Allen Point Road.

Harpswell's moniker reflects the area's English roots. It was named after the Harpswell of Lincolnshire, England, in 1758. Just a stone's throw away from Bath, Maine, this is an old seafaring and shipbuilding town. Skilled joiners were just as comfortable building ships here as they were raising barns. The overlap is readily apparent in one structural detail: "ship's knees" braces.

In timber-frame construction, a knee is a natural section of wood that incorporates a right angle or a slightly obtuse one. A branch will often grow off a tree trunk, or a root will flank off a stump in a roughly 90-degree angle. When sawn out of the larger timber, these braces are naturally strong and make excellent reinforcing members since the grain is continuous throughout. A little knee history will give us some perspective. Ship's knees were common items used in boat and ship building years ago, as was stated in *The American Marine Engineer* (1906):

> *Sturdy Ship Knees in Use Since Noah's Time*
>
> *Noah, as the first mariner, is said to have started the industry in ship knees. He discovered that the tough bend where root and tree trunk join was the best thing to brace the timbers of his ark and guarantee a safe voyage through the flood. Afterward, if not sooner, the Chinese and the Egyptians used the same system in shipbuilding, says the Washington Star.*
>
> *The invention of iron vessels with steel supports brought about a change, and today the picturesque ship knee trade is becoming a relic of the past. The State of Maine, which used to turn out ship knees by the million, now does a comparatively small business; and one must search the New York water front thoroughly before coming across a ship knee merchant's yard. There are only four or five such merchants. Maine has only three dealers in these once indispensable goods.*

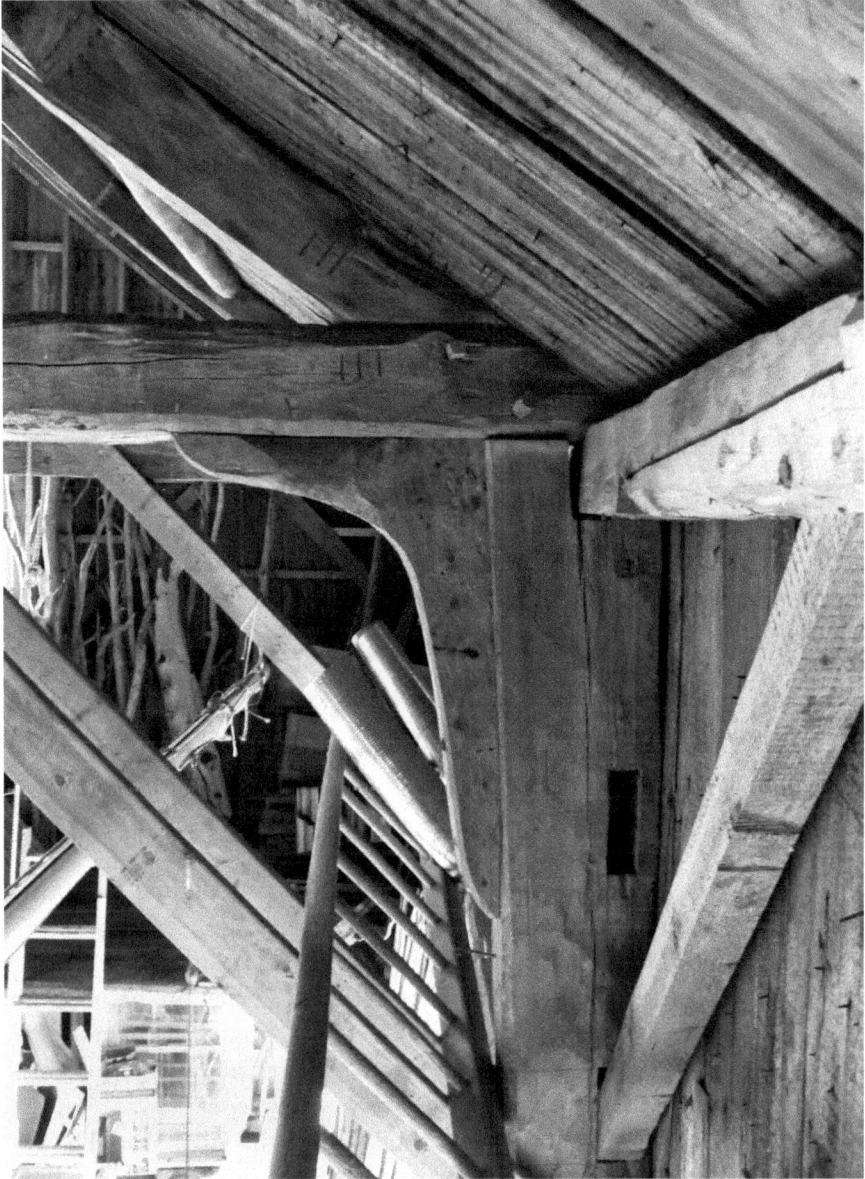

Note the carpenter's marks that are visible in the timbers, indicating a frame of traditional scribe-rule joinery. The empty mortise in the post is a mystery. It could be a mistake, a timber that was salvaged from another barn, or it could indicate where a piece from a temporary platform was occasionally inserted.

Barn owners Hank and Heidi Thorburn outside their early to mid-nineteenth-century Harpswell barn. The couple enjoyed strolling down its central aisle during their wedding ceremony.

In barns, ship's knees are often located near the tops of posts and help brace perpendicular members.

One thirty- by fifty-foot barn off Allen Point Road belongs to Hank and Heidi Thorburn and sports fourteen-foot jowled posts that are topped with English tying joints. There are twelve ship's knees among the hand-hewn, six-bent frame. There are two basic knee sizes in this barn: twenty by twenty-four and twenty-two by thirty-six inches.

The barn is old, likely having been built before the Civil War. Though no records dating construction are available, the details suggest it was built around 1850. Roman numerals can be found on the frame at prominent joint locations and is clad in wide vertical boarding that exhibits the straight saw marks of the sash (water powered) saw. The barn has a common purlin roof system. An interesting detail found in a few area barns is a slightly narrow width. At thirty feet eight inches wide, this barn is slimmer than most barns built around the same time.

Our Barns

The Thorburns are carpenters who specialize in historic remodeling and renovation, and they take pride in rehabbing old barns and homes throughout the mid-coast region. Hank Thorburn rebuilt the cupola on this barn himself a few years ago. And when he and Heidi tied the knot, they chose to have the ceremony in the barn's central aisle. (Barns' stout frames and soaring space naturally evoke permanence and growth, making them country cathedrals. On that note, a few people have asked me if I had any recommendations on barns to get married in.)

"Hank and I use the barn all the time for all different things," Heidi said, "Nothing better than to decorate it and share it's beauty and space with family and friends on our wedding day. It worked wonderfully. We even kept some decorations up for conversation pieces."

An old picture lists this property as the "Clark Farm." The cove at the water's edge just a stone's throw away is called Clark's Cove. The Thorburn brothers purchased this property from William Clark in the 1920s. The barn's original cupola is visible in the image as is an old shed, which has long since been removed, along the barn's left-hand side.

The ship's knees in this barn are bolted to the frame and are not the sole means of bracing. Regular, pegged braces, some of which are hewn and not sawn, are located in the same plane as the knees. Thus the knees are a bit ornamental rather than structural. Perhaps they were installed to reflect the area's shipbuilding heritage, or they could have been fastened specifically to "over build" the frame. Whatever the reason, the knees serve as wonderful additions to this fine barn and testify to its quality construction.

Just inland from the Thorburn barn, across Allen Point Road, is a rather plain-looking barn that belongs to Gail Hart, who has lived there for only a few years. Don't let this barn's plain façade fool you; marvelous artistry is found within.

The house and barn were built by shipbuilder Emore Allen in the mid-nineteenth century, which explains how Allen Point got its name. The parcels of land here once went shore to shore across the peninsula, and like many others, this was a saltwater farm, used for raising sheep, cattle and chickens. Today, Hart uses her ten acres of land and the barn for her goats, chickens and guinea hen.

"Several neighbors who are all related to Emore Allen loved when we started using it as a farm again," Hart said.

Like the Thorburns' barn, this barn has English tying joints at the top of fourteen-foot-long jowled posts. The barn also features ship's knees but has more than the Thorburns' barn and ones that are larger. Some are 8.5 feet

Gail Hart and her son Jaremy Parks Lynch outside their Harpswell barn, which was built by a nineteenth-century shipbuilder. "The barn, with the ship's knees in its framing, was one of the deciding factors to buy this property," Hart said. "There is nothing like being in the barn in the dead of winter, hearing the wind howl as the snow flies and feeling safe in its protection."

long by 32 inches wide while others are 5 feet by 26 inches. The two sizes are used in tandem and are bolted together in opposing and inverted pairs to help support the roof while also bracing the structure against racking. It is simply one of the most interesting barns I have yet encountered.

"The barn with the ship's knees in its framing was one of the deciding factors to buy this property," Hart said. "In late April, barn swallows arrive and take up residence for the summer. If given a choice, I would live in the barn as well!"

Measuring 32.5 by 62 square feet, the barn is a bit narrow and has been added to. Originally comprised of five bents, two more were added sometime in the late nineteenth century. The main aisle is 11 feet wide. Up in the loft, knees are found flanking either side of the main aisle posts, and bolted to the backs of these is another knee measuring 8.5 feet long that rises to meet a major roof rafter. The knees are circular-sawn.

An unusual and striking array of ship's knees. The knees display circular saw marks that date them to post-1860. These were costly items in their day; it would have been interesting to see these one-piece braces being sawn from their respective tree trunks.

It's difficult to say with any certainty what kind of wood the knees are made of, but it appears to be a softwood. Hackmatack, sometimes called tamarack or larch, was commonly used for ship's knees since it is close grained and strong, with the tree exhibiting a sprawling root system perfect for the purpose.

In 1854, at Boston's Gosport Navy Yard, oak ship's knees were offered in what was called the "Ship Stock Market." That year, knees were available from timber that was between seven and twelve inches thick. The longest dimension of a knee was referred to as the body, as it came from the trunk of the tree, while the shorter dimension was called the "arm" and was the root or branch flanking from the trunk. The largest knee available at the 1854 market had an eight-foot body with a six-foot arm and sold for $21 (about $560 in today's currency. Although no direct comparison is available for Boston, hackmatack knees were 10 percent less than oak in a New York price list from the same period.)

With four knees per bent and seven bents total in this barn, supplying the necessary twenty-eight knees would have been a considerable expense, prompting the question as to why the builder or owner chose this configuration. As Harpswell was a shipbuilding town, knees were likely readily available in the area. Nearby Bath was one of the largest wooden shipbuilding areas in the world at the time. According to an old issue of *Scientific American*, eighty-seven vessels (more than one a week) were constructed in Bath in 1854.

Perhaps some knees were left over from another boat project and appropriately priced? Or did Emore Allen simply want to flaunt his status as a shipbuilder? In any case, Allen surely could have saved money by resorting to regular timber for bracing. In some instances of timber framing, a builder chose to use ship's knees because they did not intrude into interior living space like traditional sloping braces. In a barn such as Hart's, it's unlikely that was a deciding factor.

Another point to ponder is the mill that sawed out these knees. With two-and-a-half-foot arms on the largest knees in this barn, a saw blade that was at least five feet in diameter would have been required. Precisely how the knees in this barn were sawn is unavailable to us, but an account from a 1917 edition of the *Timberman News* describes how the practice was carried out at a mill in Oregon with a special circular-saw carriage designed for the purpose:

> *There is one sawmill in Oregon designed for the exclusive milling of ship knees. A specially constructed saw carriage necessarily had to be installed for this purpose. The stump is placed on the carriage and after being lined up properly, is given four cuts with a double circular saw rig, after which the knee is ready for the pile. The sawing of ship knees is a severe ordeal for saw steel. In most cases it is almost impossible to remove all gravel adhering to the stump, and often the saw will encounter stones that are completely encased in the twisted fibers of the root. Eliminating the source of difficulty imposed by the gravel and grit, there still remains for the saw a severe test in cutting through the tough fibers of the stump.*

POWDERHORN FARM:
STAYING IN THE FAMILY: BETHEL

Along the Intervale Road in Bethel sits Powderhorn Farm where two barns from entirely different centuries are joined. The Haines family arrived after the Great Depression in 1937.

When I first visited seventy-year-old Peter Haines here, he spoke in a straightforward manner, one typical of a native Mainer.

"You lived here all your life?" I asked, genuinely.

"Not yet, I haven't," he said matter-of-factly.

On July 9, 1940, Peter Haines was born in this very house. "We farmed dairy cows and ate deer meat," he said.

The home, built by a Revolutionary War veteran in the early 1800s, is the only surviving Federal-style, hip-roofed home left in Bethel. The first location Captain Amos Powers had selected for his homestead was closer

Keeping it in the family. George and James Haines stand outside their Bethel barn, which has stylistic elements from two completely different eras.

to the river. In 1785, an area flood called the "Pumpkin Freshet" struck the region with a raging torrent, and the river spilled its banks. (The flood gets its name from the fact scores of pumpkins in the flooded fields were sent hurtling downstream.) Not wanting to suffer a repeat of this calamity, Powers had this house and barn built farther up the hill next to where the Intervale Road passes today.

The Androscoggin River begins in New Hampshire and traverses about 175 miles before reaching Merrymeeting Bay in Brunswick. It has a reputation for floods that caught early settlers unaware. Even whole barns were swept away on occasion. In *History of Maine* (1832), W.D. Williamson writes about the end of this mighty river, specifically at what came downstream and ended up at the falls in Brunswick: "The water in the freshets not infrequently rises in the river twenty feet; and in 1814 immense damage was done by the uncommon flood which brought down mills, barns, masts, logs and trees, over the falls, in undistinguished ruin."

The old gable-entry barn is a veritable fortress of hand-hewn timber; English tying joints made from oversized timbers measure between eight by nine to eight by ten inches square. Carpenter marks at joint locations indicate a scribe-rule frame. The frame is firmly reinforced by hand-hewn braces that sit on a four-foot run, which means that they are mortised into the wall plate four feet from the nearby wall post, a healthy distance. The roof is steep for its age and location, and its slope rises ten inches for every twelve inches the roof runs.

The frame measures thirty-eight by fifty feet today but was a bit longer in its original days. The stone foundation still testifies beyond the barn's current dimension.

Peter's brother George was also born in this house, arriving two years after Peter. In fact, all four of the Haines children were born here.

"My mother wouldn't go to a hospital," said George, who lived on the property until 1969. He now lives just down the street. George remembered milking cattle with his brother Peter in the old barn when they were kids. They had about ten cows they called "milkers." The family sold to Riverside Farm in Bethel. George said the barn was cold in the winter and hot in the summer. The farm was a diverse, mixed-use operation, not only used to produce milk but also to harvest potatoes, corn and dry beans.

In 1956, when the two sons were in their early and mid-teens, their father died at the early age of forty-five. Four years later, the young men decided to add a modern "tie-up" to the southeast-facing side of the barn and continue dairy farming. Under the tutelage of their uncle, the boys learned carpentry, and the trio built the addition themselves. Peter and George continued to work as carpenters in their adult lives. Sadly, like a handful of others during this book project, Peter passed away before these pages went to print.

A 1960s barn is considerably different from its forebears, and the configuration of the barn at Powderhorn Farm is a prime example. Built on a slope, the old barn had a manure basement, large hayloft and wooden floor—none of which would transition into the new cattle tie-up. In order to combat disease, newly adopted regulations called for cement floors where hoses could effectively clean them of pathogens. Hay was kept in the old barn where the calving area was located, so there was no need for a hayloft in the addition. Because of the topography, the addition was dug into an uphill slope. Constructing a manure basement was not possible, nor was it necessarily advocated as further awareness about disease transmission mandated that manure be handled differently (usually outdoors in a separate pit or other enclosure).

Of course, construction practices were quite different than they had been a hundred years ago. Concrete replaced a stone foundation, and light studding with nails replaced a pegged, heavy-timbered frame.

The new tie-up measured thirty-six by thirty-six square feet. The brothers had about twenty cattle they milked twice a day.

Modern regulations, however, brought new challenges.

"The milk inspector came every four months," said George. "He didn't like our water."

Since the outset of the Pumpkin Freshet days, neither the farm nor the barn had ever had a well of any kind. Instead, water was supplied using a lead pipe that started in a brook up on the hill across the road. The channel went under the road and divided into the house and barn.

"It took a lot of water for twenty head of cattle," George said. "In late summer, there sometimes wouldn't be much water. Sometimes the pipe would get a hole in it. I remember as a kid, [my] father would walk up where the pipe was until he found a wet spot and dig it up. He had pieces of cedar eight or ten inches long with a hole drilled right through. He cut the pipe at the hole, slid the cedar over one end and then fit the pipe on the other. It leaked a little bit, but the cedar would swell up and stop the leak."

A modern drilled well wasn't installed until 2005.

George and his older brother had little knowledge about running a commercial milking operation in the 1960s. They simply learned as they went. In 1963, after milking cows in the new tie-up for a few years, they stopped putting milk in cans and installed a modern bulk tank. They sold

Implements from days gone by and a few milk cans still hang ready for use in the old section of this Bethel barn.

milk to Breau's Dairy in Rumford at this time. George said the dairy put all of its suppliers on bulk tanks. Many small operators felt the expense was the straw that broke their backs and decided to get out of the business entirely.

"That's when we built the milk house at the end of the tie-up here," George said. "Shortly thereafter, we joined the Dairy Herd Improvement Association. A fellow would come around once a month and test the milk for butterfat and tell you which cows were doing the best. He had a truck with a body on it that he did his work in. He'd sleep in it too. He stayed overnight because he wanted to check samples both night and morning."

George's commercial dairying days were short-lived, however. In 1964, he joined the army. In 1969, Peter got out of the dairy business altogether and sold the cattle before he leased much of the farmland and started selling hay. He was an avid tractor buff and filled both barns with antique tractors that he liked tinkering with. He went full-circle and passed away in the very home he was born in on January 13, 2012.

Today, the farm and barn remain in the family thanks to James Haines, Peter's nephew and George's son, the third-generation Haines on the property. James remembered accompanying his uncle in haying and recalled a few hayrides.

"One time, we were coming up the cart road with a wagonload of hay," James said. "The trailer was mounded right up, and I was riding on top of it. Some of my earliest memories were playing in the barn and haying with him."

Organic Dairy Farmer at a Crossroads with His Beloved Old Barns: New Vineyard

Randall Bates is a real barn guy working in and out of barns every day. He, with the help of his daughter Allison, operates Springside Farm, an organic dairy in New Vineyard located just north of Farmington. Bates, who is in his mid-fifties, owns two farms and is doing his best to make the old nineteenth-century barns his family has worked out of for generations operate in today's modern-farming environment.

Sixty-four acres make up one of two parcels on Springside Farm, and the property includes a forty-two- by sixty-foot freestanding barn that his great-grandfather once worked out of. This barn is very well built, having six bents and an offset door, which indicates that it was constructed before the Civil War. The barn is used largely for hay storage and housing young stock in his dairy herd. Calves are also born here. The other barn is on a farm just up the street on 480 additional acres that have been in the family for generations. His herd is housed and milked here. Bates's daughter lives here and is helping her father run the operation.

The buildings at this second and larger location give new meaning to the term "connected farmstead." A configuration of attached buildings includes at least two barns as well as the farmhouse. Altogether it's a football field in length; there is 303 feet of sprawling building.

"All I've ever known is old barns," said Bates, adding that farming is all he's ever wanted to do. "I don't ever remember a time when I didn't want to farm. I like my independence."

That may sound ironic since Bates must milk his cows twice every day. The last time he went on an honest-to-goodness family vacation was two

Randall Bates stands in front of the early to mid-nineteenth century barn in New Vineyard where his great-grandfather worked years before.

years ago, when he managed to get away for four whole days. It had been nine years before that. Like any dairy farmer, he is absolutely tied to his milking schedule. "Generally I have them on at 6:00 in the morning, and I like to have them on again by 4:30 in the afternoon," he said.

To build up his farming operation, Bates, in addition to milking, worked on the "outside" both full time and part time for twenty-three years. He's glad he is able to simply farm today, an occupation he began in 1981 with one milk cow and three heifers.

Of the three barns that he owns, several similarities are found in their construction. They are all connected-girt buildings (meaning they lack English tying joints and do not have continuous wall plates), and the wall posts are square rather than jowled. The barns exhibit housings at the joint locations, which indicate the square rule technique was the barn's design and assembly. As such, there are no Roman numerals at the joint locations. The frames are all hand-hewn. Perhaps the most interesting detail can be

The joinery inside this Freeport English barn displays direct connections to medieval England.

A New England barn stands at Shaker Village in New Gloucester. The new design, which features the main entrance at the gable end instead of the eaves wall, was better suited to a new land where climate and farming practices were different.

From the outside, this Harpswell barn belies the fact that it is comprised of two buildings. A new roof and siding were added after the buildings were drawn together.

This circa 1840 detached barn in Sebago belongs to former Congressman Tom Allen.

The Temperance Barn, built circa 1830 in Bridgton, is so named because not a drop of rum, the traditional accompaniment at nineteenth-century barn raisings was had. Notice the offset door, which is a common feature on pre–Civil War Maine barns.

1880

An old majestic in Milo from 1880. These big, stately barns heralded a new era of prosperity, technology and the long march toward farming's commercialization.

Above: With a ramp and multiple floors, this old majestic in New Gloucester is what's known as a high-drive bank barn.

Opposite top: Built around a hand-hewn frame, this old majestic in Hiram is one hundred feet long. Early owners raised dairy cattle. Its current owners do not own livestock, but they do sell hay and keep scores of square bales inside.

Opposite bottom: Covered in slate, this old majestic in Milo is protected from the elements by one of the most durable roofing materials ever put into practice. Slate quarrying was a large industry in this part of the state years ago.

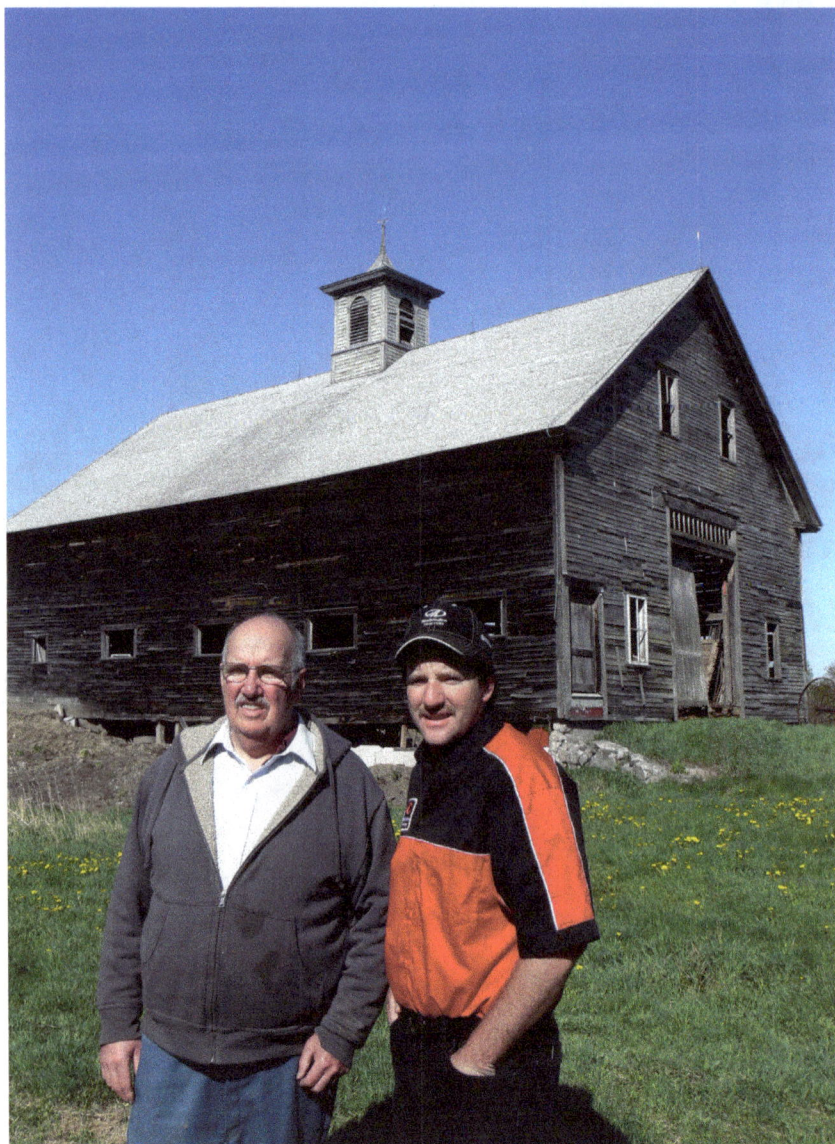

Above: Carmel Morin and Ryan Tripp of New Gloucester aren't letting this old majestic succumb to the ravages of time.

Opposite top: Years ago, the mammoth barn at Grassland Farm in Skowhegan was the first in the area to get electricity. Its recent owner recently saved this barn from an electrical fire when he happened to fetch a tool from the ground floor. He saw flames running along some wiring.

Opposite bottom: The transom window below the roof line is a telltale sign that this Searsport barn was once an early English barn.

Above: Built circa 1898, this barn in Caribou sports a hand-hewn frame, a traditional method that remained popular for years in isolated sections of Maine, such as up north in "The County."

Opposite top: Barn owners Hank and Heidi Thorburn outside their early to mid-nineteenth-century Harpswell barn. The couple enjoyed strolling down its central aisle during their wedding ceremony.

Opposite bottom: The original barn at Powderhorn Farm (on left) in Bethel is tinged in different shades of red. According to its current owner, "barn red" paint was purchased in different quantities over various periods of time, and the supplier "kept changing the formula." At right is the "modern" cattle tie-up, put on in the early 1960s.

Above: A barn with its original wood-shingle roof is a rare sight indeed. This big gambrel barn at Cyr Plantation must have been stunning back in the day when it was freshly painted. One could likely see for miles after climbing the ladder affixed to the roof.

Opposite top: Potato houses in The County were built into the side of a hill in order to take advantage of the Earth's natural insulation. Most of these houses feature gambrel roofs.

Opposite bottom: Lawrence Lord's Farm Museum on "The Airline" in Alexander. Painted old iron tractor seats grace the walls with the names of area farmers from the past and present.

The old Machias Lumber Company barn in Wesley hasn't changed much over the years, save for a center door that now appears covered over. Like many Washington County barns, this one is sided completely in cedar shingles and has no roof overhang at either the gable or eaves. Roof trim is straightforward and practical.

Dump trucks are dwarfed beside the long warehouse-style barn that was originally built in the 1970s in Edmunds Township. Because of modern hay baling practices, barn haylofts are not required on today's farms.

The sun shines bright on this big circa 1915 gambrel barn at Smiling Hill Farm in Westbrook. Gambrels are the third and final generation of traditional wooden barns in Maine.

Cattle still reside along Route 1 in Saco. This nearly ninety-foot barn sits on 125 acres of hay field.

Above: This early nineteenth-century barn originally stood in Minot. In the year 2000, Scott Hatch disassembled it, cataloged the pieces and re-erected it for his home in Harrison.

Opposite top: The Windham traffic circle, known locally as "The Rotary," came to town in 1950, five years after Stanley Hall had this big white barn built. Losing both parents by age eleven, Hall went on to make a name for himself in agricultural circles in Maine and beyond.

Opposite bottom: Note the "man door" within the larger entry doors of this barn in Arundel. Older barn doors swung on hinges. Sliding doors were a later adaptation. Some propose the idea was borrowed from railroad car patents of the mid- to late 1800s.

This barn in Gorham met its match one July day in 2008 when a thunderstorm with a powerful microburst caused this building to be lifted completely off the ground before crashing back toward earth. Its cupola shot off like a champagne bottle cork.

The aftermath. Who are you going to call if this happens to your barn?

Why not the roof? Beautiful bracing graces the hand-hewn framing in this old barn. Bracing of different types is frequently found in floors and walls but is much less seen in roof construction. The builders went the extra mile here.

seen in the roofs, which are all purlin systems. The roof boards are applied vertically. What's notable is the intricate bracing found in the roofs of these barns. Bracing is not always found in a barn's roof. In fact, it's the exception. Because of the similarity found in details of all three of Bates's barns, it's highly probable they were constructed by the same builder.

The bracing connects roof purlins to the major rafters found above the wall posts at each bent. The braces come off the major rafters and connect to an oversize purlin, which were made larger to allow for mortises that accept brace tenons. Each oversized purlin accepts four braces; these purlins are staggered throughout the roof field. Roof bracing in a connected-girt frame helps the entire structure and not just the roof resist racking. The lack of a continuous wall plate makes a connected-girt frame more prone to shifting.

Bates likes the barn at his house, which is also in the best condition. "I like where they put it," he said. "It works well with this setting. It's compact and is an easy barn to work in. I also like being associated with the history of it. My great grandfather worked it for many years. I also got to see the sunrise every morning when I milked in it."

There's plenty of romance within, but Bates admits to shortcomings in using old barns like these for modern farming. He grew up and witnessed many changes in the industry. His elders farmed, and he learned much about the old methods from them, like waiting to hay until July when those warm, dry days are upon us. Now it's widely recognized that the earlier hay is cut, the more nutritious it is, and it even allows for a second or even a third cutting in a season. Hay handling and processing has changed over the decades as well, moving from loose and square bales to round bales in just over a period of about forty years (1940s–80s). Additionally, dairy processing and storage also changed considerably in that time.

When I visited Bates, I remarked that round-baled hay is essentially a "barn killer." Since it's shrink-wrapped, it can stay outdoors all year long. No barn loft is required. He chuckled and said there is far less labor involved with round bales. "I call square-baled hay a man-killer," he said. Bates said the real "barn-killer"—what put a lot of farmers out of business—occurred in the late 1950s and early '60s, when the dairy industry switched from cans to refrigerated bulk storage tanks. "That literally took thousands of farmers out," Bates said. Another hardship was the requirement of cement floors. Unlike the relatively rapid phasing in of bulk tanks, there is not a clear-cut time frame for when farmers began covering up or replacing wooden floors in their barns with concrete. Bates said that farms that had milked on a wooden floor between the 1950s and 1970s were not required to change. However, those that were exempt from cementing their floors were still penalized every year by the state, and the industry pressured many to change. If there was ever a break in a farm's milking, milk was not allowed to be sold again until a cement floor was installed. But because a cement floor could be hosed down and cleaned far easier than wood could, cementing the floor helped to mitigate disease. Bates's grandfather walked the line and shipped milk out of the long connected farmstead on a barn floor that was half cement and half wood.

These days, Bates's barns are inspected by both state inspectors and third-party inspectors contracted by the organic cooperative he belongs to. Organic Valley sells Bates's milk to Stonyfield Farm, who puts it into yogurt. When asked how his barns are working for him, Bates reluctantly admitted, "Not very well." He sees a time coming when the old barns will be unfit for modern livestock practices. "Farming is constantly evolving," he said. "My dream barn, which doesn't resemble any of these barns, is a greenhouse barn with what's called a 'bedded back.' It's light, it's airy and the cows have freedom of movement."

However, that's strictly the business side of Randall Bates talking. He loves history and enjoys having it right at hand in his old buildings. "When I go into an old barn, I can picture what took place there one hundred years ago," he said. "I can see the people working; I can see the hay being brought in...and I can take that a step further. When I'm out on the land, I can see it being cleared, I can see the walls being built [and] the barn raising. I can see the harvest going on. I can see it all."

BIG BARN HOUSES UNIQUE ELEMENTS: WISCASSET

One particular barn in Wiscasset has everything you would expect from a barn and more. It's big, it's painted red and there are cupolas with weathervanes that point skyward. There are various additions and add-ons, too. It's simply a beautiful specimen that's seen a lot of history, and with a recent restoration where every detail was attended to, it should see many more years.

Located on Churchill Street, the farm was a dairy until the 1930s, and it sold its milk directly to customers. A few pieces of nostalgia from that era—milk cans, bottles and seals marked "Willow Lane Farm" to name a few—have been saved in the barn's old tack room. Besides dairy, there's plenty of evidence that this was a horse barn. Ten horse stalls in the main barn are located along the building's south and sunny side. The horse stalls have beautiful iron railings and are paneled in rich tongue-and-groove woodwork. Flanking the main barn on either side are two additions. One joins the house and is the original barn on the property. Built with hand-hewn timber, it dates to the early nineteenth century and possibly earlier. On the far side of the main barn is where the dairy cattle were located. Early twentieth-century regulations driven by disease factors often mandated that horses and cattle be kept separate.

And there's more. An old milk house that is separate from the barns still stands a few feet away. A 1931 calendar from the Wiscasset Grain Company still hangs within.

Claudia and Dan Sortwell smile happily in front of their Wiscasset barn, which has been in the Sortwell family for generations. Absent of animals today, the barn works nicely for the couple's small but growing coffee roasting company.

Animals are absent from the property today, and the old cattle tie-up has been retrofitted for a more modern purpose: coffee roasting.

Dan and Claudia Sortwell operate Big Barn Coffee, a business they started here in 2009 after acquiring and restoring the property from Dan's parents in 2007. However, the farm has been in the family for several generations, starting in 1735 when Robert Foye acquired the property.

"We sell coffee at four farmers' markets," Dan said. "The coffee roasting room in the barn is just great. The high windows allow a lot of light to come in."

The Sortwells are active in their community and use the rest of the barn for meetings and various public events. It's a very clean and beautiful space with a few different time periods all under one roof.

The big gambrel-roofed barn in the center of the complex measures forty by seventy-five feet today, but it was originally a bit smaller, measuring only forty by fifty feet. The gambrel-style roof is a dead giveaway that it was built in the twentieth-century, and the interior, where one can readily see the construction details, reinforces this date range. Gambrel-roofed barns are the third-generation style of barn found in Maine. Like most gambrels, the barn is a mixture of timber and stud framing. Its walls are made up of circular-sawn six- by six-inch timbers at major joint locations with two- by four-inch pieces of lumber spaced in between. These studs sport an unusual spacing of eighteen inches. The roof is comprised of circular-sawn two- by six-inch pieces of lumber that do not register directly above the wall studs. These are spaced on twenty-four-inch centers. The six- by six-inch timbers are widely spaced at sixteen feet apart, and the main joints are pegged.

This is a classic example of an early twentieth-century barn where builders were transitioning between two eras of barn construction: traditional timber framing and modern "stick-frame" construction.

The top floor of this section is almost completely boarded over and was mounded with loose hay years ago. A section immediately above the main aisle is open, and it once allowed hay to be hoisted to the second floor loft. An old hayfork mounted to a track running the length of the building still hangs from the roof's peak.

"As a child in the 1950s, I remember when they would hay here," Dan recalls. "It was loose hay. We used to go up to the loft and play."

There is a small wooden-framed structure that resembles a phone booth on the floor over the horse stalls. This was the hay chute that allowed a man to pitch hay down to the animals below. Although the chute is still accessible, leaving it open would cause loose hay to cover and block the chute's opening.

Originally, Dan and Claudia contemplated a wide range of uses for this barn, including the possibility of showing movies up in the hayloft. However, local fire codes proved problematic, and the idea was soon scrapped.

Dan's father grew up here, and Dan said his grandfather had several horses. Some were used for work and some for riding. While I was inspecting the barn, I discovered a feature that I had not seen before. There was evidence that iron drain pans had once been connected to plumbing drains. Apparently, years ago, horse urine was used in the manufacture of gunpowder. As it is inherently high in ammonia, horse urine makes volatile gunpowder mix and was often substituted for water.

The old cattle tie-up in the addition farthest from the house joins to the main gambrel roof at a right angle. When standing in the main barn one can see old wood shingles between spaces in the roof boards here, testifying to the original roofing material.

Both the floors and walls in the old cattle tie-up are finished in concrete, making it easy to clean, and this feature works well for the Sortwells'

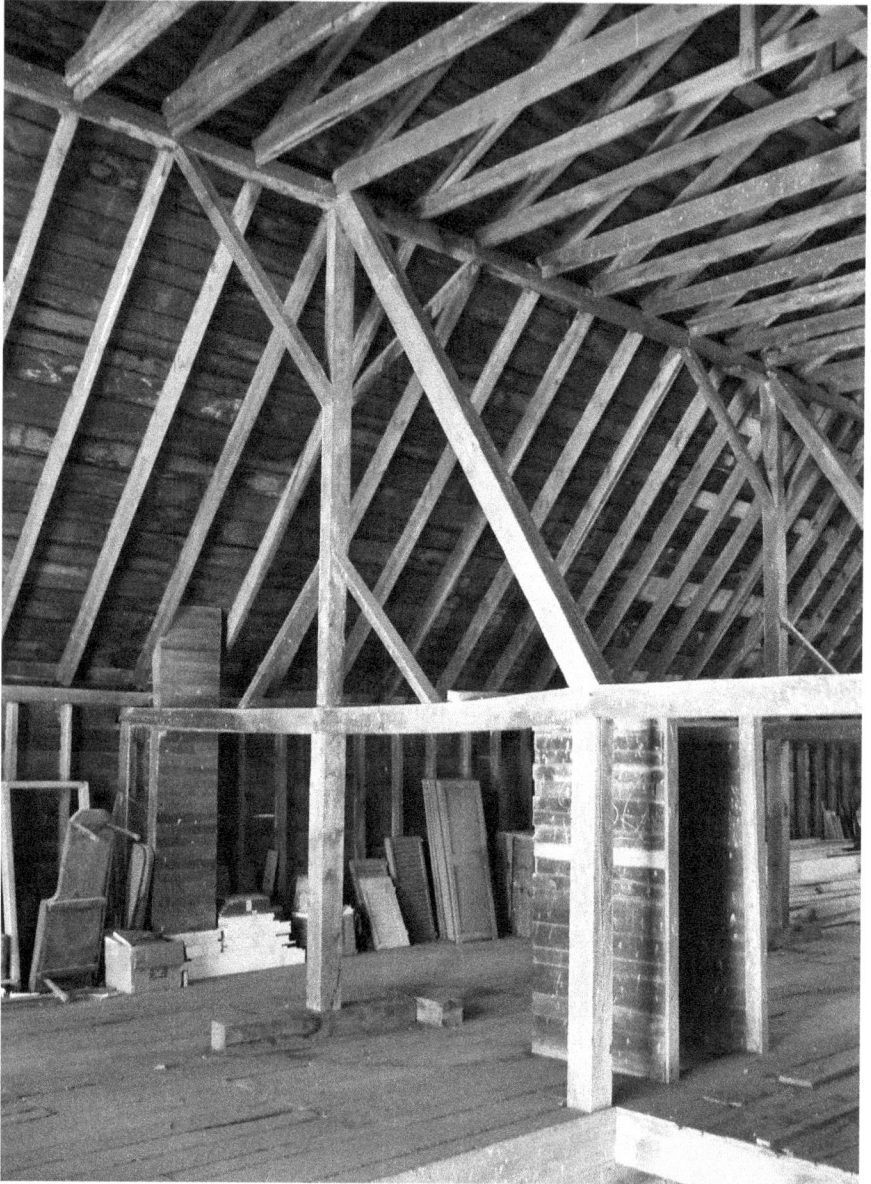

When the loft of this barn was full of loose hay, this enclosure allowed someone to stuff forkfulls of hay through an opening down to the horse stalls below.

Providing a comfortable yet workable and disease-free surface for cattle was a challenge. Surrounded by finished cabinets today, this floor contains a special brick, a kind of rubberized asphalt, that cattle stood on when this was a tie-up for hours on end.

coffee roasting today. An interesting detail in this section is on the floor. Surrounded by a field of concrete, a relatively hard, rubberized asphalt-type brick sits where the cattle were once held. It is worn from time and use, but Dan said it is comfortable to work on. Several materials were historically used for floors in cattle tie-ups, including many types of brick (such as cork brick).

An old text entitled *Dairy Cattle and Milk Production: Prepared for the Use of Agricultural College Students and Dairy Farmers* (1911) by Clarence Henry Eckles dates to around the time this barn milked cattle:

> *One of the most important points to be considered in planning a barn is the material to be used for floors. Material for a floor should have the following characteristics:—[sic]*
>
> *1. Impervious to moisture.*
> *2. Sanitary and easily cleaned.*
> *3. Comfortable for the cows.*

4. First cost not too great.
5. Durable.
The floors in common use are as follows: Dirt with wood or cement gutters.
Wood. Brick. Cement or granitoid.

The barn looks beautiful today thanks to the restoration work of Tim Hanley, who repaired the house after it suffered a fire before Dan and Claudia moved in. There are forty windows (eighty sashes), which were all redone locally in frames of Spanish cedar. The Sortwells decided to use the old and original wavy glass panes. These were fixed in their frames with stainless steel glazing points.

"Set up in what's now the coffee roasting room, it took a worker all winter to glaze the windows," Dan said, adding that the old windows were not a standard, off-the-shelf size found in today's catalogs. They required a custom fit. Using the original glass helped offset costs, and Dan said he likes the wavy look of them.

Another example of high-quality construction is found here on the barn's main entry doors. They slide easier than any you're ever likely to encounter.

CHAPTER FOUR

UP NORTH AND DOWN EAST

The Border Barns of Aroostook and Washington Counties

A t the northernmost tip of the Pine Tree State is Aroostook County, a vast area about the size of Connecticut. "The County," as it's called, is a region still very much defined by its agricultural heritage. The County has nearly four times the farmland of York and Cumberland Counties combined. Almost 400,000 acres are under cultivation in the potato capital of Maine.

The County at a glance:

YEAR	FARMING ACREAGE	NUMBER OF FARMS	AVERAGE FARM SIZE
1940	793,218	5,706	139 acres
1974	448,090	1,561	287 acres
2007	375,568	1,246	301 acres

Total area: 6,671 square miles

In The County, the potato is king. According to the USDA, potatoes were the state's top agricultural commodity in 2010. Dairy and aquaculture trailed respectively. Spuds have been a commercial crop in Aroostook since about 1890 when area farmers produced $1.5 million that year. Forestry on an industrial scale is another large interest.

In 1902, Clarence Edgar Pullen wrote about the proliferation of the potato in his travels to The County in his book, *In Fair Aroostook*:

A great and constant demand for the Aroostook potato is for seed in the Middle and Southern States, and of the 1,009 carloads of potatoes shipped by the Robinson Company [Presque Isle] 150 carloads went for seed to 18 different states extending from Pennsylvania and Ohio southward to Texas. The seed potatoes are carefully selected and assorted so that only the variety desired shall be sent in response to an order—for of varieties of the potato in Aroostook there is no end. In a list that Mr. Robinson handed me are 27 varieties.

The County is unique to the rest of the state. Instead of a primarily English lineage, most folks emigrated here from French-speaking Canada (which explains why no one here has a Maine accent). Many from southern Maine have never visited this region of the state. Additionally, The County has always been an area packed with pride. Late nineteenth-century visitors remarked positively upon seeing the area's agricultural pursuits, which was voiced in an excerpt from Maine's *Annual report of the Bureau of Industrial and Labor Statistics* (1897):

There is no section of this State or of New England that has handsomer farms, finer farm buildings, or neater looking villages than the Aroostook of to-day. The houses are as well furnished in every respect, as they are in any section of our country. There are more organs and pianos in the homes of Aroostook people, than in an equal number of homes in the remainder of the State.

In the way of barns, the gambrel roof is a predominate feature in those found at Aroostook. Most barns have this roof style, reflecting a combination of ethnic influence and the region's late settlement (as compared to the rest of Maine). Compared to other parts of the state, Aroostook is far from the coast and does not have many rivers, along which most of Maine's tiny villages and traditional mill towns sprouted up. Military concerns over a disputed international border with Great Britain in the nineteenth century ultimately ushered in a road network that allowed easier access to the region.

Aroostook County was incorporated in the 1830s. Some two hundred years earlier and three hundred miles to the south, York County was incorporated in the 1630s. The names themselves illustrate the counties' stark differences. York is obviously of English origins whereas Aroostook is a Native American name.

Not only is the language different up in The County, but the soil and forests are too. Unlike central and Southern Maine with their time-honored stonewalls, you'll have to look far and wide to find a rock wall along many of Aroostook's fields. Moreover, folks living up "in the crown of Maine" probably wonder why Maine is called the Pine Tree State as pines are very much secondary to the spruce, fir and cedar of northern forests. Instead of oak trees, the maple leaf that flies on Canada's flag is much more at home.

Before potatoes became the primary industry, lumber, like most of Maine, was what drew early settlers to Aroostook, as described in this passage about shingles in *History of the Lumber Industry of America* (1907):

> *In 1878 a writer, noting the passing of the pine of Maine, said: A generation ago Aroostook County was known only for its shingles, rived and shaved by hand, from the vast forests of cedar. The stumpage didn't cost anything, for the shingle-makers stole it, and by hard work they could earn fifty cents a day...Cedar is as plenty in Aroostook as bristles on a hog's back...A very considerable part of Aroostook's logs are cedar and pine for shingles, the Van Buren Shingle Company alone having cut 10,000,000 feet in the 1901–2 season for the supply of its mills at Van Buren. Aroostook shingles are known all over the New England states and beyond as of fine quality; and, as the supply of cedar is very large, the industry is likely to continue indefinitely and with increasing success, owing to improved transportation facilities.*

The St. John River served as the international border, where Aroostook's early settlers lived and floated lumber out of the woods. The town of Madawaska was the first permanent settlement in Aroostook. Established by the French in 1785, these folks were the descendants of Acadians the English had driven out of Nova Scotia years earlier. More French from Québec eventually came to join them as Clarence Albert Day explained in *Farming in Maine 1860–1940* (1963)

> *Here they lived for several decades in almost complete isolation, while their settlement spread out in either direction along both banks of the St. John. They had very little intercourse with the English in New Brunswick...and none at all with the Americans in the rest of Aroostook.*

A generation later and some one hundred miles south of Madawaska, the first English-speaking Aroostook settlers came from Massachusetts, arriving at Houlton in 1805. The town is named after Yankee land surveyor Joseph Houlton. Among other settlements between the two towns are the communities of Mars Hill, Presque Isle, Fort Fairfield, Caribou and Van Buren. Instead of vast fields of potatoes and other crops, the wooded western section of the county is largely commercial forestland.

OLD WAYS ENDURE IN AROOSTOOK: CARIBOU

Just north of downtown Caribou along Route 1 is the barn of Clarence and Juliet Plourde. One of the first things a barn scholar will realize about The County's barns is that they are almost always gambrel-roofed and detached from the house.

Clarence Plourde was born in the farmhouse here, and his grandfather had the barn built in 1898. It measures twenty-nine by forty-one feet, an odd size that doesn't fall neatly on a modern tape measure.

"I was born here in 1924," Plourde said. "We had everything; we had dairy, beef, pork and chickens. If we slaughtered a cow or pig my mother was up at four o'clock in the morning making sausage. She made just about everything."

Potatoes were always grown by the family, and like nearly all pre–World War II farms, there were no refrigerators. Plourde said they had a small outbuilding, an icehouse, where meat would naturally freeze in the winter.

"After it got too warm to keep things frozen, my mother would salt the meat or we'd buy ice," he said.

Plourde's father would go see a man in nearby New Sweden to get ice. Cakes of ice were brought home and put in the icehouse, and everything got packed in sawdust.

"He was the only one on this road who used to do that," Plourde said of his father.

Years later, long after electricity brought year-round refrigeration, Plourde's own daughters played in the old icehouse, calling it their dollhouse.

The barn has a somewhat unique layout, incorporating main doors on the eaves walls as well as a large pair at a single-gable end. The building has been added to over the years with additions and lean-tos, but the core barn has its main aisle (twelve and a half feet) along the eaves wall. Another set of doors used to be located as an exit on the other eaves side, suggesting more

Built circa 1898, this barn sports a hand-hewn frame, a traditional method that remained popular for years in isolated sections of Maine, such as up north in "The County."

of an English barn layout than a New England or Yankee one. At each side of the main aisle are fourteen-foot bays. The hayloft is quite large, and its gambrel roof design maximizes space. The most efficient roof shape is a domed roof, and some barns, particularly those built after World War II, have trussed, dome-shaped roofs. A gambrel is the most practical way to arrive at a dome shape using straight lumber. Most of the gambrel-styled barns in Maine were built after 1900, generally making the feature a dead giveaway as to the barn's age, especially in southern parts of the state. The design gained much popularity between the first and second world wars. It appears Aroostook County may have started using this design a little earlier than the rest of the state.

Lots and lots of loose hay led to the creation of this roof style. Plourde said he didn't begin using baled hay until about 1950.

"We didn't have a baler," he recalls. "But there were some around, and we hired one along with some young men to help. We had a pulley up in the

A major purlin marks the transition and midway point on one side of this barn's gambrel roof. The gambrel is the predominant style for Aroostook County barns. Note the hand-hewn brace at left. Every piece of this frame was crafted with axes.

barn roof. It's still there. We would tie six or seven bales together and pile them just about to the peak."

Plourde farmed all of his life. After coming home from World War II, he continued the mixed farm operation his parents had started, which included selling milk and butter. Plourde soon transitioned to breeding beef cattle and ultimately began harvesting potatoes full time. This barn saw it all. Initially working with his brother, the pair farmed about 35 acres of potatoes. Decades later, Plourde was farming about 125 acres of potatoes on his own and maintained a few potato houses. These structures also had gambrel roofs and were built right into the side of a hill. Like a root cellar, the surrounding earth helped preserve the contents inside. A woodstove prevented the spuds from freezing in the winter.

Hand-hewn, pegged eight- by eight-inch timbers compose the frame of Plourde's barn, and the building only uses four bents. The discovery of this time-honored technique in a 1900s barn surprised me. It's rare to find a gambrel-roofed barn in southern Maine that's built with hand-hewn timber. Indeed, it's unusual to find any barn of this relatively late era framed with hand-hewn timber. One really does have to travel the state to get a complete picture of its "barnscape."

There are no flared posts or English tying joints in Plourde's barn, and being in French-Canadian country, I didn't expect any. However, like the major timbers, all the braces in the frame are hand-hewn, a surprising detail usually found on much older barns.

Indeed, everything in the frame is hand-hewn. Perhaps a sawmill was too far away or its products too expensive for Plourde's grandfather, who ultimately decided to log his land and provide the builders with homegrown stock; perhaps everything was hewn onsite.

Like nearly all barns in Aroostook, the roof framing is a common rafter system. These rafters are basically half-round, peeled poles spaced about two to three feet apart. Halfway up each side of the roof is a large hand-hewn purlin running the length of the barn. There is no ridgepole.

One thing of interest in this and many other Aroostook barns are the roof and wall sheathing, which are circular-sawn on Plourde's barn. The boards are relatively narrow. Large pines that yielded wide boards for barns in southern sections are not as plentiful here in The County. The sheathing is likely spruce or fir, which is typically a much narrower tree.

The roof is a section Plourde has to keep his eye on.

"We get a lot of snow in this part of the state," he said. "If you get a rain with the snow already there, that adds up to a lot of weight. I've seen as much as six feet of snow on this barn."

It's not uncommon for Plourde to hire someone to clear the barn's roof. But despite being in his eighties, Plourde gets up to shovel some sections of his house that aren't as steep. Originally, the barn was roofed in wood shingles. These can still be seen between gaps in the roof boarding when you gaze up from inside. A few layers of asphalt shingles have been added over the years. Other telltale signs of modernization include a cement floor that Plourde installed after he transitioned to potatoes full time. Another point to note is the general lack of manure basements among the barns of Aroostook County. Plourde's is no exception. By the time this barn was built, knowledge of disease transmission resulted in the feature falling out of favor. Originally, the barn's floor was wood. Plourde said machinery came here after World War II.

Agriculture modernized quickly after the war and many farmers disliked their old barns. Interior posts, beams and low ceilings were often not well

Clarence Plourde, a retired potato farmer who is now in his eighties, still lives in the house he was born in. He can be seen shoveling his own roof in winter from time to time.

suited to the new tractors and modern equipment. For more room, Plourde removed a post in the middle of one of the center bents. To shore up the beam, he installed long pairs of two- by six-inch braces that extend to the exterior wall posts. Many farmers altered the framing of their barns after World War II. Some, like Plourde, realized they needed to install alternate supports. But many farmers simply hacked away at their barn frames with the buildings suffering as a result.

I asked Plourde why most of the barns here in Aroostook are detached from the house. He didn't have a very clear answer: He simply stated that they didn't want it that way. In fact, when asked if he thought a connected barn was a good idea, he quickly said no.

"There was one barn down here years ago," he said, pointing south toward town, "that was connected to the house, but it was torn down… That's the only one where the barn was connected to the house."

Plourde continued to explain that the only reason a barn and house were ever connected was to save going outdoors to tend animals in the winter. This is a common belief but one that's not entirely accurate. As Tom Hubka pointed out in his book *Big House, Little House, Back House, Barn: the Connected Farm Buildings of New England* (1984), areas like Minnesota and Wisconsin have winters equally as severe as Aroostook, as does upper New York State. However, you won't find connected barns there. Though there are a few connected barns in Aroostook, they are not the norm. Like Plourde's, many of Aroostook's barns were built after the connected style had fallen out of favor. Many factors encouraged detached barns. Modern building and fire codes, insurance regulations and disease considerations were the largest factors. A connected barn is a terrible thing should a fire ever break out.

"We just didn't want a connected barn," Plourde said. "There was no need of it."

Though Plourde wasn't around to see this particular barn being built, he does remember other barn raisings, which he and others in the area refer to as "a frolic."

"Most of the farmers would come and help," he said. "I remember—I was small but I saw it—they'd put a log on benches and with axes they'd make an eight by eight out of it. Can you imagine? Those guys must have been pretty smart."

He's right about that.

Upon visiting these northern barns, all of which are located in an isolated area full of hardworking people, the notion that the old ways of barn building continued into the twentieth century here in Aroostook is clearly reinforced.

AN ACADIAN EXAMPLE: CYR PLANTATION

Between Caribou and Van Buren sits Cyr Plantation, an unorganized township way up north in Aroostook County. Along Route 1 is a grand old barn that must have been simply stunning in its day. The barn was built in 1933 by the LaPierre family and has an amazing intact feature: an original wood-shingled roof, a rarity in any locale.

At sixty acres, this was a true "homestead farm" from the Homestead Act. This farm is not active today. The forty-five- by sixty-five-foot barn was built during the Great Depression. Dan Deveau, the prior owner of this barn, grew up next door and said most of the area's barns were built during this time.

"The top of the barn was for loose hay," he said. "They had a small area for livestock and chickens; it was an all-around barn."

And what a barn it must have been. Though no longer being actively used and nearly devoid of paint, the barn would have been a beautiful sight when it was gleaming white. A fancy, arched window still graces the peak.

Deveau is an avid historian and has insights into the gambrel design that is so prevalent among barns here. He has listened to elders talk about barn raisings.

"You had one guy, the bee-liner, with a straight eye," he said. "Others who weren't afraid of heights were climbers. And you had those who were good with an axe, the hewers. Everybody had their skills. The pictures that I've seen had fifty to seventy-five people that usually came. The men would work and the women cooked for everybody."

According to Deveau, many of the Acadians who settled here were skilled shipbuilders. Though none are present in this particular example, a few barns in the area display ship's knees. Deveau points out that many of the region's barns resemble upturned boats, especially when examining their framing. Early on, he said, the Acadians built gambrel-styled barns, while those from Québec typically built regular (gable) roofs.

The skill is evident from the interior's design. At forty-five feet, the barn is quite wide and is made from a mixture of sawn and hewn timber. The most notable example of skill is in the tie beams, which are hewn members, spliced at the building's center. These beams are mostly hewn square but are essentially round where they splice. Why a single hewn timber was not used is unclear. Perhaps several forty-five-foot timbers were difficult to obtain. The wall plates are also spliced.

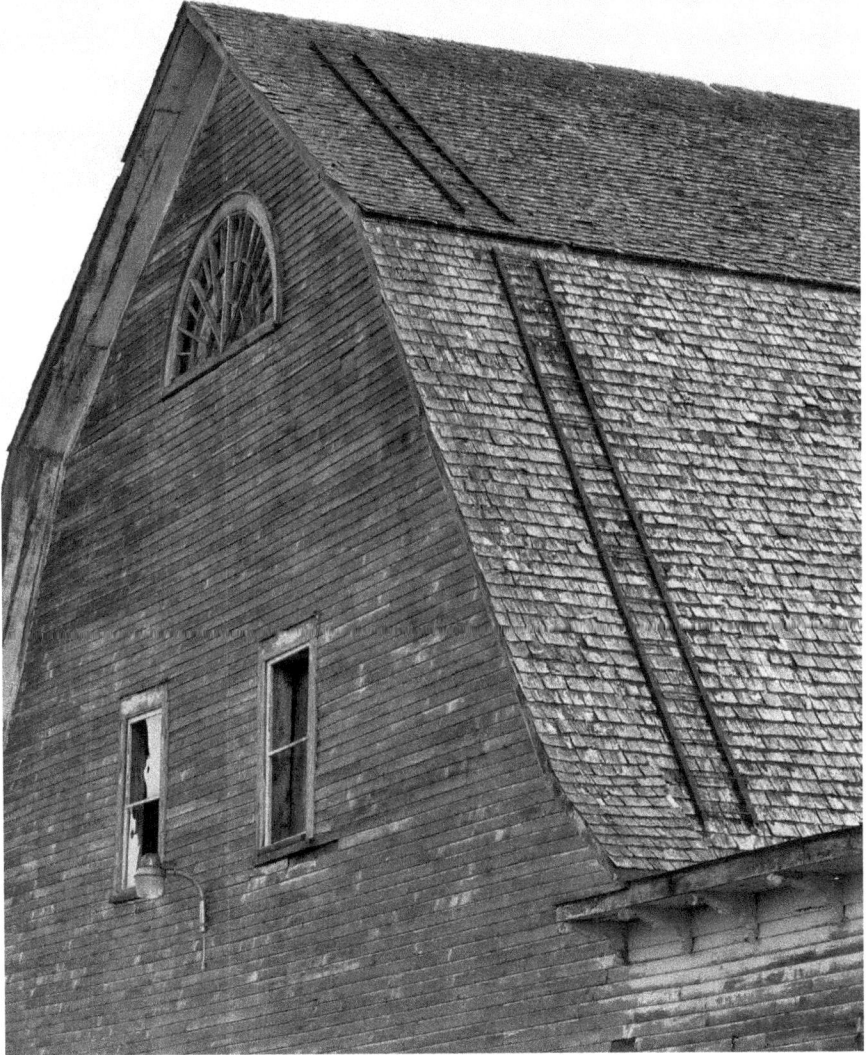

A barn with its original wood-shingle roof is a rare sight indeed. This big gambrel barn must have been stunning back in the day when it was freshly painted. One could likely see for miles after climbing the ladder affixed to the roof.

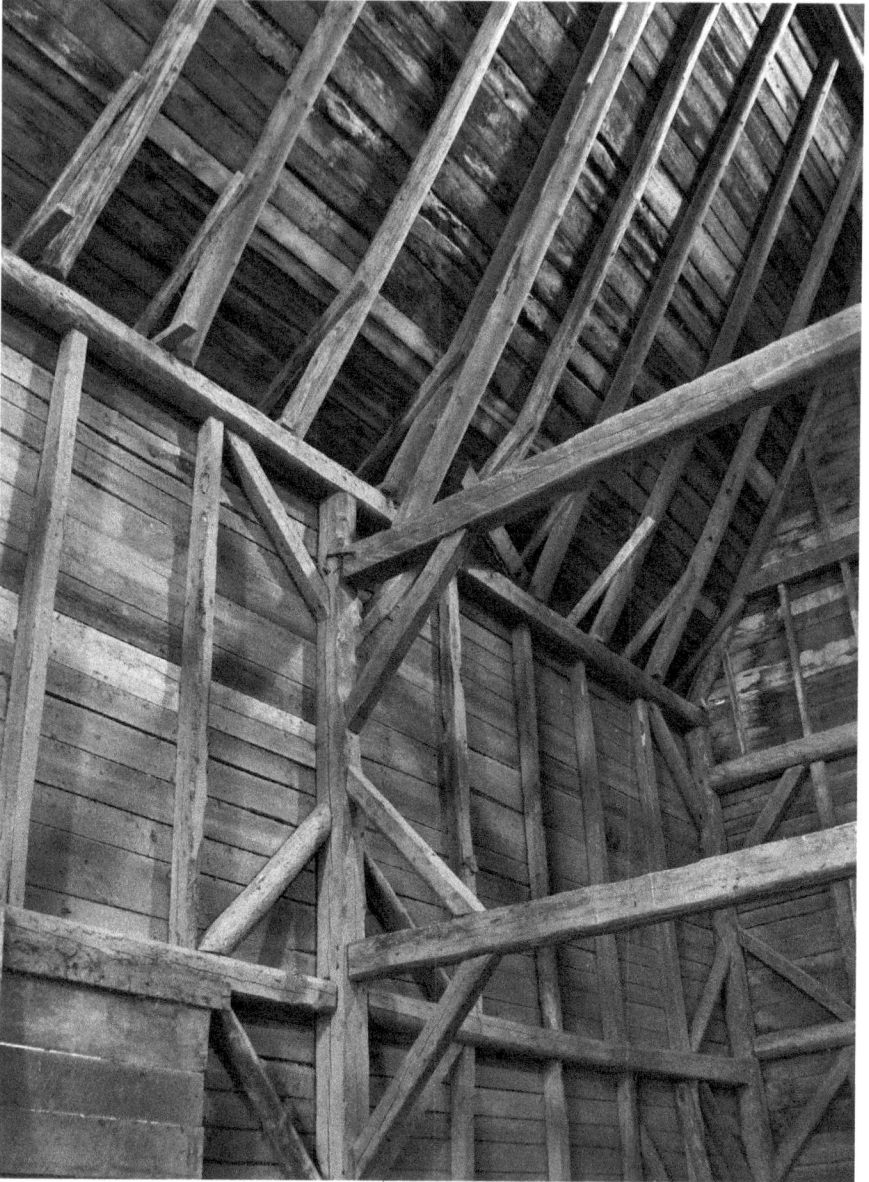

This circa 1935 barn in Aroostook County reveals a mixture of hand-hewn and circular-sawn material. The dropped tie beam appears to be the standard method in The County.

Working with round material is inherently more difficult and is one reason why logs were squared into beams in the first place. To make a splice in a round log is more difficult than it is in a square beam. However, it's a balance; hewing is arduous work and leaving part of the timbers round likely saved a bit on labor.

Times soon changed following the Great Depression, and this barn was not used for farming for very long, perhaps fifteen years. After World War II, farming practices shifted, and horses and the mounds of hay they needed were replaced by mechanization and gasoline. The building became primarily used for equipment storage. The post–World War II era also brought increased specialization on a single crop (potatoes in this neck of

Dan Deveau stands outside the wood-shingle roofed barn in his section of Cyr Plantation. Mr. Deveau knows much of the area's history and says the area's barns were built by the Acadians who come from a long line of shipbuilders. "These barns look just like an upturned ship inside," he said.

the woods) and planting and harvesting used machinery instead of horses. You can still see the horse stalls in the barn, however. Along the south side, ten feed doors testify to where the farmer would have fed the animals hay. On the far end, three cow stanchions still remain.

In the middle of the barn is its wider-than-average, fourteen-foot main aisle. The north bay is fifteen feet wide. There are no windows along this side, which is a dead giveaway that this area was the haymow. Besides the arched window at the front gable, two dormers peek out along the middle of each roof slope, letting in much-needed light. A single metal ventilator graces the peak.

Despite some broken windows and neglect, the sixty-five-foot barn is still in good condition and only uses five bents that are spaced sixteen feet apart. However, it is well braced and has studding between each bent. This studding provides a nailing surface for the horizontal boarding. Like the walls, the roof is also horizontally boarded. Peeled-pole rafters on three-foot centers make up the roof framing. Like the Plourde barn examined earlier, large purlins running the length of the barn define where a change in roof pitch occurs.

POTATO HOUSES

If you travel The County with an eye for barns, it won't take long before you notice many unique looking gambrel-roofed outbuildings stuffed into hillsides. These are potato houses.

Most of them were constructed in the early twentieth century. Basements and root cellars typically kept spuds throughout the winter before this. A traditional potato house was normally empty in the summertime.

One oddity that is immediately apparent when studying these is the presence of a brick chimney just like one found in a home. A potato house is perhaps the only "barn-like" outbuilding where a wood stove is housed within. Though they are becoming something of a rarity nowadays, it's possible that you still might see a potato house chimney puffing smoke on a back road in The County—a telltale sign that it's still being used for its original purpose.

Like a scene from the past, an old potato house near Caribou puffs smoke from its chimney during winter. Though perhaps not considered a true barn, these outbuildings were once common in The County and are likely the only agricultural outbuilding with a chimney where a wood stove kept the potato crop from freezing and excessive dampness during winter.

PARKHURST SIDING ROAD

In the town of Presque Isle along the Aroostook River is the Parkhurst Siding Road where you can find a thirty-six by sixty-foot potato house that was built circa 1915. Built into the side of a hill, this potato house, like most others, borrowed design principles from high-drive bank barns of the late nineteenth century. Gravity did some of the work. Potatoes were brought in directly at the top level, which is typically at the rear. Wooden potato barrels were rolled along the upper floor to the appropriate dumping place, and loose boards or trapdoors could be opened with potatoes then dumped into the bins below.

When it was time to ship the spuds, the lower doors on the opposite gable end were opened where a wagon or truck typically backed up for loading. Potatoes were shipped by rail in the early days. This potato house was used until about 1980.

Potato houses in The County were built into the side of a hill in order to take advantage of the Earth's natural insulation. Most of these houses feature gambrel roofs.

Instead of a central location, a chimney is found on the front left-hand side, which seems to be the usual spot for them in this area. Firewood was added to a woodstove on the bottom floor perhaps every couple of hours in the wintertime. Other than the surrounding earth, most potato houses were not insulated, although Clarence Plourde of Caribou remembered a layer of straw about a foot deep spread on the upper floor of one of his potato houses kept some heat below. The interior of a potato house was never room temperature nor was it ever intended to be. A woodstove was there simply to keep the potatoes from freezing, as well as drying out the humid space. A wood or metal ventilator at the peak assisted in drying out the interior.

In construction, most all potato houses are stick framed. The one at Parkhurst Siding Road has heavy timbers framing the first floor, but the roof is comprised of common rough-sawn rafters that are two by six inches and clad with narrow, horizontal boarding.

THE AMISH: FORT FAIRFIELD AND EASTON

When do you suppose the last barn raising happened in Aroostook County—1915? 1925? 1940? Well, it was 2012, and more barns have been raised during the preceding years. These aren't fancy "barn-like" buildings intended for some wealthy person to keep a collection of prized convertibles in. No sir, these are honest-to-goodness working barns that are full of animals and were built by the Amish.

The Amish first visited here from upper New York State around 2005, hoping to survey a new area they could relocate to. In 2007, a couple of families put down roots in the town of Fort Fairfield and neighboring Easton. Now there are about a dozen families in the area.

"The availability of good quality farmland, friendly people and the welcoming nature of the towns of Fort Fairfield and Easton, as well as other things like the beauty of the area, were what helped us decide to move here," said Noah Yoder, an Amish carpenter living in Fort Fairfield.

And move here they have. The Amish are nothing if not industrious. They have taken small, abandoned or unused farms, the kind unattractive to corporate-scale agriculture, and made them prosper again.

"When we raised our first barn, we were told it was almost exactly one hundred years to the day since the last barn raising happened in Fort Fairfield," Yoder said.

The Amish barns are unique for the region; they are not gambrel-roofed. Instead, they adhere to a gable with a strict nine-in-twelve roof pitch (which means it rises nine inches for every twelve inches the roof runs).

The Amish do everything in the old way, eschewing electricity, telephones, cars or computers. They drive horse buggies and school their own children. In farming, they are like the Maine farms of years ago; rather than concentrating on a single commercial crop, they practice a mixed-use operation. Their hay is harvested by hand and is stored in the barn loose instead of in bales.

"A nine-in-twelve roof pitch is ideal for loose hay storage," Yoder said. "Anything less than [that] will reduce the height of each forkful as it is lifted off the wagon and rolls back into the mow, resulting in less hay storage. A steeper pitch will result in the hay catching on rafters as it rolls back to the haymow because the peak becomes too narrow."

The Amish do not adhere to a standard center-aisle "New England" or "Yankee" barn design. Instead, they build their barns in a t-shape that allows for large haymows on either side of the main aisle. At thirty-eight feet, the width of the barn has also been carefully calculated for efficiency. Anything wider than this causes wasted steps while doing simple chores, such as shoveling manure onto a wagon. Animals are kept in the basement level, while grain and hay are stored above. Animals are stabled on each side of a central aisle on the lower floor. The animals face the exterior walls and deposit manure toward the center aisle of the building. Anything wider than thirty-eight feet makes pitching the waste into a manure spreader inefficient since more steps are involved.

"The proportions come from the function of the building," Yoder said.

Upon first hearing that the Amish were building barns in Maine, I was filled with anticipation and excitement. I expected to see time-honored timber frames pegged together with intricate joinery. But what I found were distinct frames largely constructed of two- by six-inch timbers nailed together. The frames are clear to the peak in the center aisle, so no beams are in the way. Yoder, one of the head barn-builders for the Aroostook Amish, described the benefits of this style and why it is continually used:

"The last mortise and tenon, pegged timber-frame barn built out of new lumber that I remember our community building was in 1985," Yoder said. "It's possible that some other Amish communities may still use timber framed mortise and tenon construction, but I am not aware of any. It takes considerably more time and manpower. The method we now use has proven to be as strong or stronger. Plus it is more user-friendly for hay handling."

The heart of the barn is made from a main aisle framed of six- by six-inch purlin posts that are about twenty-four feet long. These are braced out to the exterior foundation by equally long timbers. The main aisle is about eighteen feet wide, far larger than a traditional New England or Yankee barn aisle typically found in Maine. The side bays, where the livestock is kept, are ten feet wide, which is a bit narrower than is typical for Maine. The entire roof is framed from sawn two- by six-inch rafters, and everything is nailed. The system is effective at controlling roof spread while allowing a clear span in the center aisle from floor to peak. Yoder said the construction method is not his design and is unsure just who or where it came from.

Growing up in Ohio, Yoder has been around barns and barn raisings his whole life.

"You grow up with it," he said. "Children under twelve put up roofs; I've never been to a barn raising where anyone's been seriously hurt."

Noah's grandfather built barns, and one time when he was young, Noah attended a barn raising his grandfather helped lead. A mishap occurred, but

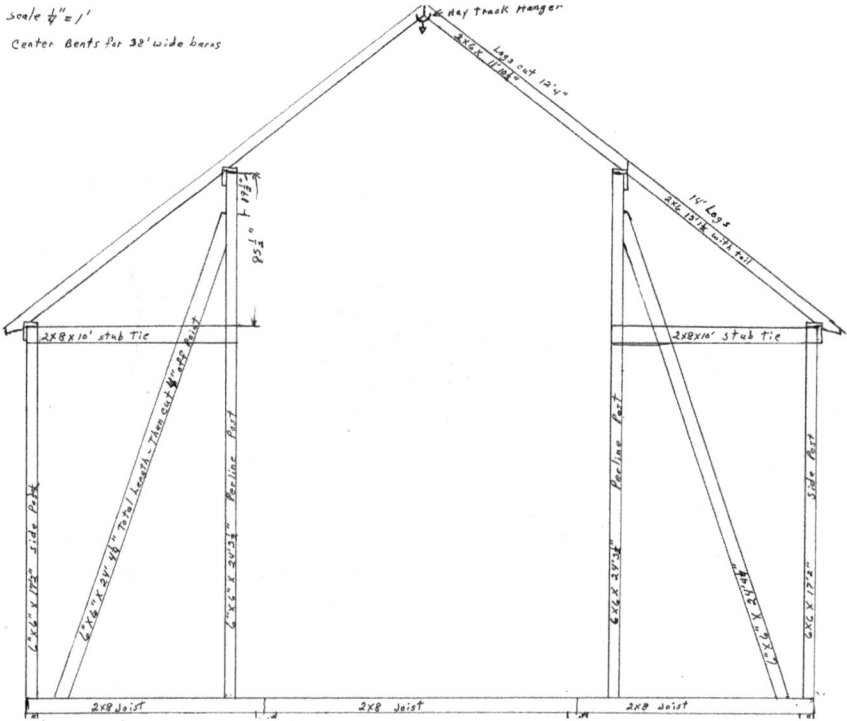

A sketch by Amish carpenter Noah Yoder shows the configuration of the community's barns. This configuration allows an unobstructed central aisle, perfect for putting up loose hay as the Amish do not use modern balers.

the consequences were not physical. Rather, the situation proved who was capable of doing a certain task and who was not. Nobody assumes a role within the Amish that they are not absolutely proficient in.

"It was a traditional, heavy-timber framed barn design," Yoder said. "A bent fell off its sill as it was being raised and slid down a slope several feet. The bent had to be completely disassembled, pegs driven out, and then reassembled. My grandfather made sure the man who was tasked with getting the post tenons into the sill mortises never did that part of the raising again."

He said there are typically about sixty folks for each barn raising. However, there weren't nearly that many available when the first families moved up here to The County. Instead, many of the Amish back in the home communities of Upstate New York came up to help. But most of them didn't realize just how far it really was. Whether you leave upstate New York

A barn raising in Fort Fairfield in 2009. Note the frame is made up of lightweight, sawn material. *Photo courtesy of PaulCyrPhotography.com.*

A barn raising in Fort Fairfield in 2009. The proportions of the building come directly from its intended use. The roof pitch is calculated to maximize efficiency in hay handling. *Photo courtesy of PaulCyrPhotography.com.*

A barn raising in Fort Fairfield in 2009. *Photo courtesy of PaulCyrPhotography.com.*

A barn raising in Fort Fairfield in 2009. *Photo courtesy of PaulCyrPhotography.com.*

and go across Canada to reenter the United States at northern Maine, or decide to travel across Vermont and New Hampshire, it's still a distance of over five hundred miles. But that didn't deter them. After milking their animals one evening, scores of Amish boarded a bus for the drive to Maine, raised Yoder's barn, got back on the bus and were back for the next day's milking schedule. Not bad at all.

DOWN EAST: WASHINGTON COUNTY

Washington County is the easternmost region of Maine, (and America, for that matter) and is a region referred to as "Down East," a term from old seafaring days when Boston mariners navigated eastward to Maine ports. Pushed by southwest breezes, these ships sailed downwind. Thus, going "Down East" meant sailing to Maine.

At the end of the line, so to speak, the area's relative isolation preserved far more than a Down East accent. The barns in this region also stand as a testament to the area's early inhabitants. The first permanent settlers were almost exclusively English, hailing from Massachusetts and southern Maine. The major industries here were, and continue to be, lumber, blueberries and fishing. Another notable industry is Christmas tree and wreath production, as the area is loaded with spruce and fir. The St. Croix River makes up the eastern-most border of the United States, and according to the writings of George J. Varney, the river witnessed the first European sermon ever given in New England.

Machias is the area's county seat. Those of English descent settled here in a peculiar circumstance in the 1760s after forest fires had ravaged New Hampshire and western Maine. In *History of the Lumber Industry of America*, James Elliott Defebaugh quotes a passage accounting the event that pushed southern Mainers increasingly Down East:

> "[In the autumn of 1762 an expedition, consisting of the settlers from Black Point and Scarborough, was made to the extensive marshes on rivers east of the Penobscot to obtain hay.] *Another object also was to explore the places they visited for the purpose of setting up a lumbering establishment. For the fires before alluded to had destroyed a great portion of the pine timber lands in the vicinity of*

Scarborough, and, being in the habit of lumbering more or less every year, they [the settlers above referred to] *were not disposed to overlook the advantages which a new country might afford for this purpose. Our little exploring expedition, in their progress eastward, at length arrived at Machias, where they found hundreds of acres of marsh, covered with, to them, invaluable grass...And here, too, their keen, practical observation discovered a wilderness of untouched pine timber forests, overhanging a water power of almost unlimited extent, unoccupied, and at the head of tide water navigation...On their return the story of their voyage, and of the discovery they had made, was soon told...Not a few of the inhabitants... listened with eagerness to accounts of a more favored location—of a spot where the lumberman and the husbandman could find resources of wealth so abundant."*

WASHINGTON COUNTY at a glance:

YEAR	FARMING ACREAGE	NUMBER OF FARMS	AVERAGE FARM SIZE
1940	291,163	2,358	123 acres
1974	84,517	277	305 acres
2007	35,655	472	336 acres

Total area: 2,563 square miles

The isolation of places like Far East Maine, where families were typically rooted and didn't move away until recent years, preserved English customs, including the kind of barns constructed and the joinery therein. The more I researched for this book, the more it struck me that this part of the country is called New England for a darn good reason. Many do not recognize it at first, but the term New England is absolutely a literal statement.

When you consider it, Maine's early ties to Massachusetts, which was overwhelmingly English, were very strong indeed. It may surprise us to learn that the "Maine accent" actually originates from Boston and, from there, England. The isolation of places like Down East Maine preserved the dialect for generations. Maine was a province under Massachusetts's government from 1652 to 1820, with scores of Massachusetts families coming to Maine for essentially free land. Maine has towns like New Gloucester and New Vineyard (named after Martha's Vineyard) that emphasize these connections. In Cumberland County, the neighboring towns of Gray and Windham, were first called New Boston and New Marblehead respectively.

Before this book project, I had visited Washington County just once in my life, and I was too young to notice or appreciate the area's regional details. Many years later, at age forty-two and traveling with an eye for barns, it didn't take long before a pattern appeared. English barns are the prominent barn style in this part of Maine, and it's likely that isolation is the reason. English barns were the first of the three major barn types in Maine. New England (or Yankee) and big gambrel-roofed barns respectively followed.

I traveled up the coast along Route 1 and also diverted into the interior for this book. I was fortunate to meet up with a fellow history buff who also happens to share an affinity for barns.

John Dudley lives in Alexander just off what is called "The Airline" (Route 9). John compiled a survey of barns in his town and neighboring Crawford in 1990. He knows where many of the old barns are. A member of the Alexander-Crawford Historical Society, John also contributes history columns to the *Calais Advertiser*. After early lumber exploration, John said most settlements in Washington County were encouraged largely to keep the British out of the area since the northeast boundary of the United States was still largely up to interpretation after the revolution. During the years surrounding the War of 1812, the British actually captured Bangor, Castine and Machias.

Now in his seventies, John grew up in Calais and spent summers and vacations at his grandfather's camp in Alexander, about fifteen miles west of Calais. His father had dairy cows, and John proved to be a competent escort in my quest for barns in Washington County. An avid history buff, John wrote a grant to the Maine Humanities Council in 1990 and put together an exhibit comprised of sixteen foam-board displays featuring barns in Alexander and the surrounding towns of Crawford and Cooper.

Barns in Washington County exhibit common traits. Most are plain with little or no ornamentation, are detached from the house and are built on flat ground with no manure basement. The siding of choice is almost exclusively cedar shingles. Another notable detail is that roof pitch is steeper than similar-era barns found in the southern part of the state.

How do we know the barns here are English? Besides a style dictating the barn's main entry doors be placed along the eaves wall, the joinery also has its tales to tell. English tying joints are found in the larger barns of this region. As previously mentioned, this joint configuration has its origins in thirteenth-century England and remained the standard in barns among those of English descent for over five hundred years.

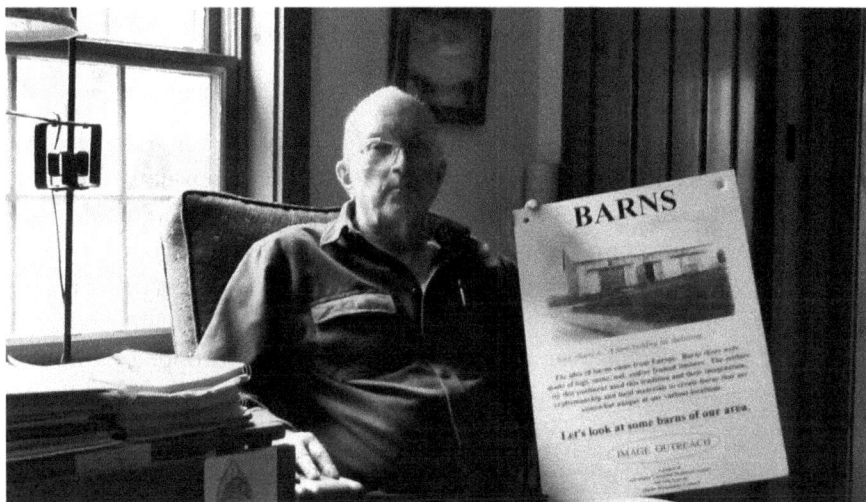

History aficionado John Dudley in his Alexander home with one of several foam boards he put together illustrating the area's barns.

Farming has never played a major role in Washington County. Lumber was the predominant industry, with shipbuilding emerging a little later. Besides river settlements, early industrial activity centered around its many and dependable tidal areas where tide mills provided necessary and abundant power for sawmills. A proximity to seaports and convenient shipping were also close at hand. As a result, inland settlements were small and scattered; a trend that continues today. Washington County was much larger than it is today. In 1839, Aroostook County formed and siphoned off much of Washington's northern region.

The larger barns here exhibit hand-hewn frames with English tying joints. Smaller barns are almost invariably built of smaller timber in the five-by-five- to six-by-six-inch range and display different joinery configurations than the English tying joint. These are composed of "H-bents." (The tie beam is dropped a foot or so from the top of the posts, which resembles the letter "H.")

It's always nice to have a guide in unknown territory.

"Barns were disappearing," John Dudley said. "As a local historian, I wanted to make a record of the past."

Folks viewed his foam-board exhibit at the Alexander school, Alexander Grange Hall and the Calais and Woodland Public Libraries. John took me around to see many of the barns depicted on his 1990 display. A few have succumbed to the passage of time and are no longer with us, but we visited four that still stand.

The first one is a hip-roofed barn in Meddybemps that is owned by Dennis Gillespie. This is a hand-hewn frame with dropped tie beams that are reinforced with iron dogs, a kind of large iron staple strengthening the post and tie-beam connection. The barn is almost square, but evidence points to a few remodels over the years. For instance, the roof is not original; the first was undoubtedly a gable with the eaves over the main doorway. Two opposing walls have small cripple studs above the dropped tie beams to create a common plane for the feet of the newer hip roof rafters. Some old jowled posts, likely from a barn with an English tying joint, have been put into service in the interior. These hold up the tie beams' centers at the two interior bents. There are no animals here today. A nice cupola sits at the apex of the roof. Dating the building is difficult because it is comprised of reused elements from different time periods. It does not date before the Civil War since circular-sawn studding is found nailed between the major timbers. Dennis is looking into what it will take to save the structure. The bottoms of the posts have deteriorated; the next few years will prove critical to the future of this unique, freestanding barn.

A small hip-roofed barn in Meddybemps that's off the beaten path. The roof is not the original, and details inside suggest the original configuration was a typical English barn with a gable roof with eaves over the main entry. The current owner is deciding whether he should preserve the structure.

The next barn John took me to is referred to as the "Crosby Place" on North Union Road in Cooper. John said this barn dates to about 1870. The building is no longer used for animals and farming. This somewhat larger barn sports a hand-hewn frame and English tying joints. In other parts of the state, the English tying joint is not typically found after the Civil War. But isolation breeds tradition. Indications suggest builders in Washington County likely continued the time-honored practice of the English tying joint a bit later. The following passage from Solon Robinson's *Facts For Farmers* (1868) emphasizes this:

> *Necessity has done much for the building public by introducing to their favorable notice the balloon* [stud frame] *style of building wooden buildings—a style which is not well understood in the old settled and well-timbered portions of our country.*

In New England, especially isolated sections with plenty of timber on hand, barns framed from heavy timber and traditional methods happily continued.

Bent spacing is close in this barn, measuring nine and a half feet. The roof is a common rafter system. One thing of interest discovered in Washington County is that purlin roof systems are the exception and not the rule. In this particular barn, vertical wall boarding is in keeping with the tradition of early barn styles found in other parts of the state. Most barns were not sided when built, as vertical boards shed water far better than horizontal ones did.

The third stop on our tour was on the Cooper Road in Alexander at a barn referred to locally as "Nelson Flood's barn." Like the others, this barn is also empty of animals today. The original farmhouse was located across the road and burned down in 1957. A favorable wind and a "bucket brigade" of locals saved the barn. Another home was built, but it is not occupied by the barn's current owner. Not much is known about the history here, except that Nelson Flood milked cattle into the 1960s. John said a man named Lester Johnson was killed by a horse within these walls years ago.

The barn is a wonderful example of an early Washington County barn. It's been some time since it's been active. It's only when you get inside this long barn that you realize it is actually two barns that were likely hauled in place end-to-end by oxen many years ago.

Moving barns was actually quite common a century or two ago. With no plumbing or wiring to contend with and little or no building codes governing the placement of outbuildings, it was far easier to move a barn in the past

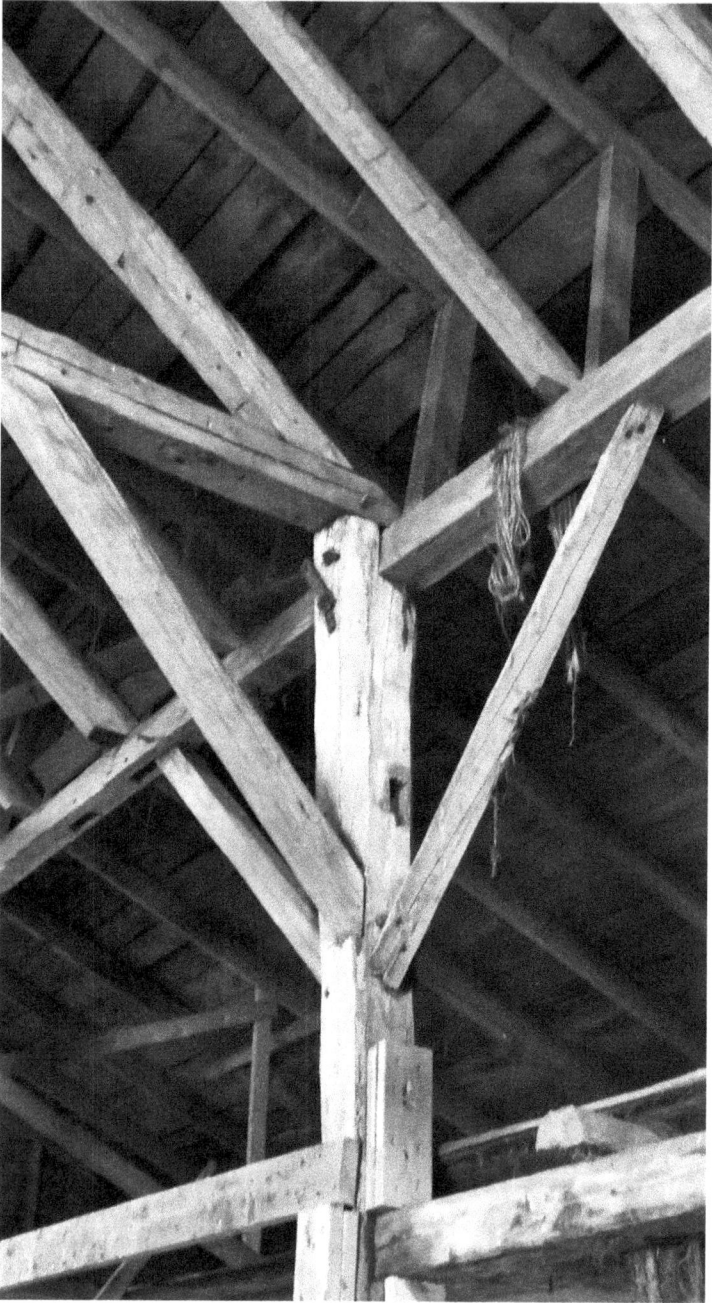

An English tying joint in a barn on North Union Road in Cooper. Note the common rafter roof system. This barn had an addition put on to its rear. Though some larger barns have them, purlin roofs are typically the exception in roof framing in Washington County.

A tale of two barns. Local historian and barn guide John Dudley stands in front of a long English barn in Alexander, which is two separate buildings placed end-to-end. The lean-to on the left-hand side was added later. Cows were milked here until the 1960s.

than it would be today. Buildings were usually hauled in the wintertime when the ground was hard and the buildings slid easier. Pictures in old books often show teams upon teams of oxen yoked together in front of buildings as they were moved from one place to the other. It must have taken a skilled crew and lots of patience.

Measuring thirty-seven by eighty-one feet, the barn is certainly long, in fact far longer than other barns of this area. Even before venturing inside, this in itself is an indication to the would-be barn researcher that it might be two buildings.

Though similar in construction details, it's not likely the barns were built by the same builder. How do we know this? By the details inside.

Both barns are comprised of hand-hewn frames with English tying joints. The differences lie in subtle details within the joinery itself. For example, the rafters are tenoned into their tie beams in the part of the barn closest to the road. In the other half, the rafters are simply spiked in place with large "trunnels," or treenails (oversize pegs) that protrude through the bottom of each tie beam. There are other details in the wall bracing. The bracing is hand-hewn in the half closest to the road, while sawn braces are in the other section. It's likely the half closest to the road is older, but this cannot be absolutely verified.

It's interesting to see how the two barns were physically joined together. About midpoint along the eaves walls, there are two posts abutting each other—the telltale sign that it is indeed two barns. It appears the movers got the barns closer together on one side than they did on the other. A gap of about four inches on one side causes the whole barn to have a slight curvature. The entire roof has been redone, as has the siding; the building looks relatively uniform today, but it would be neat to fly straight over the ridge of this barn and see the slight curvature in the roofline.

When the barns were as close together as the movers could manage, the workers then fastened the two buildings together with wood instead of hardware. A large hole about three inches in diameter was bored through both posts, and a large wooden treenail was then pounded into place. This treenail is heavily mushroomed from the beating it received. The same practice was carried out on the opposite side that didn't quite come together. In this case, the workers fitted a block in the space between the posts and drilled clear through everything before pounding another large treenail in position.

At some point in the twentieth century, the building received a lean-to on its southern side. This area is whitewashed, which is a dead giveaway of Nelson Flood's former cattle tie-up. Today, the whole barn is covered in cedar shingles, except for the roof, which is enclosed in contemporary sheet metal roofing. The entire barn has a purlin roof system, but this was altered at some point so that the newer roof boards are applied horizontally. A large hayfork still swings from the roof peak.

The layout of this and other large English barns is something to contemplate. Despite being a little over eighty feet long, there is not a main aisle stretching the length of the barn. In a New England gable-entry barn, a long center aisle is employed with animals on one side and haymows on the other. When barns became increasingly used for livestock rather than grain storage, a long central aisle was welcomed, since the farmer could service the entire length of the building with a horse and wagon without needing to turn it around. Doors on each gable end allowed easy entry and exit. By contrast, Nelson Flood's barn, with its English design, has many sets of doors found along the eaves wall. In this, the barn is set up more like a warehouse loading dock. If you want to access a certain bay, you open a certain set of doors. However, because of the lean-to added to the other side, you must exit the bay through the same door you entered. Adding a central aisle here would have been somewhat problematic, however, since a line of posts is set right in the center of every tie beam. However, a center aisle would have

The inside of the long English barn, known locally as "Nelson Flood's barn," on the Cooper Road in Alexander. Note the close pairing of two posts and the filler block between added below the two braces that is secured with a treenail (or "trunnel").

The song "A Tombstone Every Mile" by Dick Curless spoke of the dangers facing long-haul truckers on Washington County's Route 9. Here, in a barn turned museum, Lawrence Lord creates his own tribute to the area's hard-working farmers.

been possible by simply offsetting it to one side of this row of posts. Perhaps this was a little outside the box for a population whose barns had long been based on the older English layout. It is interesting why gable entry took so much longer to seep into barn design here, and even then it is far between.

The fourth and final stop on our tour was Lawrence Lord's Farm Museum, a big barn on Route 9 in Alexander. This barn is an utter fortress of hand-hewn construction, made up of slightly oversize timber. Again, English tying joints testify to the ancestry of the area. Like the Crosby Place, John said this barn also dates to about 1870, and in keeping with that barn, it also has a common rafter roof system. Vertical boarding graces the walls of both barns. These barns appear to have some shared history in their construction details.

Lawrence Lord operates a well-drilling business, but his real love is old tractors and related farm equipment. He has all manner of agricultural memorabilia housed within this barn. It's definitely worth a visit if you're heading down The Airline. Old iron tractor seats have been beautifully repainted and hang as testaments to longtime Washington County farmers. A few of the names artfully inscribed include "Hiram 'Mott' Dwelley," 1873–1963; "Foster Higgins," 1903–1978; "Clinton Flood," 1903–1986; "Joseph Lord," 1903–1988; and "Bert Varnum," 1914–2008.

A Loggers' Horse Barn: Wesley

As mentioned earlier, lumbering drove most early settlers to Maine. Before America's independence, it was the "King's Pine" that had England thoroughly absorbed with Maine. The Crown was more than willing to fight for such resources. Like other Washington County ports, Machias was under proclamation during this time, as described in *History of the Lumber Industry of America*:

> *The provision, restricting the cutting of His Majesty's timber on the township, refers to a condition in the provincial charter that all trees of twenty-one inches in diameter, upwards of twelve inches from the ground, were to be reserved for masts for the Royal navy—and a fine of £100 was incurred for every such tree cut down without a license first had and obtained of the King's surveyor.*

After immediate coastal and tidal areas were cut, timber was cut up river and floated to port. After we cut our ties with England, waterways continued to be important to the logging industry well into the twentieth century. In the town of Wesley, between the Machias and East Machias rivers, a horse barn still stands that catered to the animals that once hauled logs from the woods to the water. Horses were once found on every farm in our great state. In 1900, Maine had roughly 103,000 horses. Forty years later, that number had plummeted to just 37,000. By contrast, cattle numbers held relatively steady during the same period. In 1900, Maine had roughly 173,000 dairy cattle. Numbers dropped a bit to 132,000 in 1940.

Separate from its farmhouse, this barn was once part of the old Hayward House that catered to travelers, including workers of the Machias Lumber Company. In the late 1890s and the early decades of the twentieth century, logging crews worked along the Machias River in this region and would stop here to get a hot meal and a comfortable bed and to give their horses a rest, too. Dick Carlow lives here today and has deeds stipulating that the Machias Lumber Company purchased this property in 1919.

"My parents bought this place in 1958," said Carlow, who is now in his seventies. "My grandfather, Otis Carlow, hewed some of the beams in this barn. I was in the service for twenty years and didn't come back here until 1961. The barn last had livestock in the early '60s, but we had hens and sheep here until the '80s."

Measuring thirty-two by seventy-six feet, the building is actually two barns. However, it appears it was added on to, rather than having separate buildings hauled together. In keeping with other barns in the region, the barn has an English layout with main entry doors along the eaves wall. Each half of the barn has its own entry with a sliding door. The barn was essentially doubled in length. Though the building looks homogenous from the outside, construction methods between the two halves differ significantly. The section closer to the road sports English tying joints, while the other section has H-bents with dropped tie beams. Timbers within the whole structure are hand-hewn, and the wall boarding is vertical while there is horizontal roof sheathing throughout applied over a common rafter roof system.

Fourteen horse stalls stand along the barn's north end; cattle were kept on the south section. The names of cattle are still etched on the boarding here.

Logging is still prominent in this part of the state. Before skidders and heavy equipment, hay was in major supply and was often toted in to early lumber camps. With Bangor earning the title of "Lumber Capital of the

World" in the nineteenth century, Penobscot County was first in lumber exports in the 1840s, but Washington County came in second. In these early pre–Civil War times, oxen were used for logging as horses were considered too weak for the job. Paul Bunyan, the mythical logger, didn't use a horse but an ox. This philosophy mirrored the conventional wisdom on farms as well as forests in early times. In an interesting account in *History of the Lumber Industry of America*, James Elliott Defebaugh quotes a passage from an old-time logger reminiscing about 1850s life in the Maine woods:

> *"When I first went to work in the woods, in 1854, only oxen were used for hauling, and no one thought of beginning operations until snow had come, so that supplies could be sledded in to the camps. For hauling logs a team of from four to eight oxen was yoked to a bobsled, a short sled with a single bar upon which was placed a heavy timber called a bunk, which served to strengthen the bar and prevent its being worn out. On this bunk one end of the logs was placed and securely chained, the other end dragging, so that the team moved the load by sheer strength. Then the logs, before being loaded, had to be barked—that is, the bark was hewed off from one side, so that they would drag along with greater ease. This used up a good deal of time and has been done away with by the use of wagon sleds.*
>
> *There was no 'yarding' of logs then, as today, all logs being hauled directly to the 'landings.' To load the sled for each trip the oxen were taken from the pole and used to drag the logs upon the sled—a very slow process. The sleds and yokes were made after the crew had arrived at camp, the sleds without a scrap of iron in them except the clevis pin at the end of the tongue. The yoke bows were brought into the woods, hung to the necks of the oxen; and, for the yokes, we hunted up crooked birch trees with the right bends in their trunks and hewed and shaved them into shape. With a pair of horses and the wagon sled in use today a man can do as much work as one could in the old times with a bobsled and eight oxen. The change to horses has effected a great saving, for the men move more quickly now and little time is wasted."*

A couple of details in the passage are notable. One is the lack of hardware in those days and how nearly everything was fashioned on-site from wood. According to the Patten Lumbermen's Museum, in the 1820s, early logging camps were fashioned without nails and were simply constructed of large notched spruce logs chinked with moss and mud, usually making a square twenty by twenty feet. All the work was done with an ax and froe. The roof

Richard Carlow outside his barn with an old pulley block, which was once used to hoist hay up into the loft. Carlow said that during hunting season, deer were hoisted in the barn as well.

was made of cedar shakes held down by long poles across each tier and tied down with cedar, spruce roots and bark strips. This, to an extent, mirrors early barn construction. It's why frames were simply pegged joinery. Besides door hinges, no hardware—save nails—was used in barns well into the late nineteenth century. Hardware was expensive and simply unavailable on the frontier; early farms being no exception.

The other notable detail in the above account is how oxen were the primary means of hauling and how slow they were. However, working with horses quickly gained favor once their superior speed was realized. After the Civil War, most logging and farm chores employed horsepower instead of oxen. Because horses are taller animals, this caused barn ceilings to increase in height

According to Defebaugh, during the 1901–02 season, logging operations in the three northernmost New England states produced 1.4 billion feet of logs, employed forty thousand men and required thirteen thousand horses. Maine was by far the largest producer, with 750 million feet of logs coming from the Pine Tree State. About 15.5 million feet went down the Machias River alone that season. Getting logs to the waterways required a lot of horsepower. No doubt, the barn at the Hayward House in Wesley was an important part of operations for the Machias Lumber Company as it housed the men and horses.

Fred Hayward, a descendent of the original owners, has an old Hayward House ledger with entries from October 1895 to September 1899. Various entries list crews who stayed and boarded their horses. Geary, Ames, Gardnier and McLaughlin were some of the crewmen listed. Two meals and a night's lodging set a man back 75 cents in those days, and it cost 38 cents a night to keep a horse in the barn. October–January recorded the most entries in the ledger, suggesting these were consistently the busiest months out of the year for logging operations.

TIDE MILL FARMS: EDMUNDS

Route 1 goes right through Edmunds Township in Washington County, a coastal community that includes Coobscook Bay State Park. Just south of this is Tide Mill Farms, which has been in the family for some 250 years. Aaron Bell is the eighth generation here, and he, his wife, Carly DelSignore,

One of just three dairy farmers left in all of Washington County, Carly DelSignore and husband Aaron Bell sit at their kitchen table at Tide Mill Farms in Edmunds Township. Bell is the eighth generation to carve out a living from the family's 1,600 acres on the upper reaches of Coobscook Bay.

and their small brood of children continue a farm legacy in a world that's changed dramatically in the last fifty years. Yet some things have remained the same; the honor system is alive and well.

When I visited to see things for this book, Aaron was at home having lunch. We had talked earlier on the phone, and he said he'd meet me down at the barn. While I waited there, a man got out of a minivan, entered the barn's small office area, gave a nod and opened the refrigerator to grab a couple of gallons of milk. He then put his money in a container and left. I didn't realize it at the time, but he had just purchased two gallons of Tide Mill Farms organic milk. No receipt. No problem.

Tide Mill Farms is currently one of just three dairy farms in all of Washington County. With eighty head of cattle, half of which are milked twice a day, two modern barns provide shelter. The word "modern" is relative here; the barns were built nearly fifty years ago in the mid-1960s and early '70s. Instead of wooden posts and beams with basements and haylofts, these all-metal buildings resemble a warehouse more than a barn.

The barns were built by the previous generation and reflect a statewide trend that began in earnest after the Civil War: the steady march toward commercialization. In order for dairy farmers to make it today, they have got to produce on a commercial scale. Coupled with its inherent isolation, this is one reason why so few dairy farmers are left in Washington County.

The two metal barns are attached. The biggest is immense in size, measuring 85 by 160 feet. Metal posts support trusses measuring sixteen feet apart. There is only a single floor, and a low-pitched roof is used because hay is not stored here. Like many in the business today, Tide Mill Farms uses round hay bales that are shrink-wrapped in white plastic. These can stay outdoors all year long. Many farmers call them "marshmallows." This revolution in hay storage began in the 1980s. As a barnologist, I see these round bales essentially as a "barn killer" since they do not need to be sheltered.

Before World War II, hay was often kept loose, and large barns with haylofts were needed, despite the fact a family would have a relatively small number of livestock. This along with modern practices in manure handling, such as the absence of basements, changed barn configurations considerably in the years after the war. Another factor driving a warehouse-like structure with an open floor plan was an increasing reliance on big machinery. Years ago, once they had made the switch from horses to tractors, many farmers began to dislike their old barns. With low beams and posts interrupting the floor plan, old barns were something most commercial farmers had to increasingly "deal with" and modify rather than viewing them as beneficial assets.

For the most part these days, farmers like the big round hay bales. There's much less labor involved—they do not have to stack thousands of square bales by hand. And there are other benefits.

"What the marshmallow bales allow you to do is harvest grass at a more nutritious state," Bell said. "Instead of needing three days of dry weather in the early season, which can be difficult, you really only need one day. You just mow it and bale it."

The old saying "make hay while the sun shines," is far less applicable today. Farmers of old learned early never to put moist hay into their barn. Put away loose, the composting action of moist hay can create immense heat. Spontaneous combustion often occurred and burned barns as hay can and will ignite around 350 degrees Fahrenheit.

Aaron and Carly say doing square bales isn't all that realistic anymore, simply because the farm culture has changed. Aaron recalled producing square bales on the farm as a kid but agrees that it's different now.

"We went from a culture where kids did farm work," Carly said. "They didn't expect to get paid nine dollars an hour or need a worker's compensation policy; chores were simply a way of life. Unfortunately, that's not how things are done anymore. To find a hay crew to do square bales is nearly impossible. It makes more sense to put that money into equipment for round bales. Doing round bales makes sense since that former lifestyle has disappeared."

"It was a summer tradition," Aaron said, recalling haying in the summer. "We did square bales; it was fun. My father and his brother would have to find half a dozen crew members from the neighborhood to help."

Cattle have not been milked here continuously for generations. Aaron and his wife began milking here in 2005, nearly thirty years after the previous generation stopped and transitioned to marketing wood and hay off of their 1,600 acres. The organic milk market has made dairying viable again. Aaron said the barn needed significant capital to upgrade its milking system and to drill a new well, but he likes the nearly forty-year setup, which is what's known as "loose housing."

"With loose housing, the cows are milked in a parlor," he said, "whereas 'tied stall' requires you to bring the equipment to the cows and install a network of plumbing in the barn. The barns here work really well."

CHAPTER FIVE

SURVIVING IN THE SOUTH

The Barns of York and Cumberland County Farmers

T he southern part of Maine is well known for the Maine Mall, the state's largest airport and turnpike widening. Some feel it is not really Maine. But our southern region still has many barns, including some of the state's oldest. Generally, it's very tough to find a barn anywhere in the state that dates before the mid- to late 1700s due to the French and Indian War (1754 1763) that burned much of the frontier of Maine and delayed future settlements.

Maine remained an edge of civilization long after places such as Massachusetts and Connecticut were fully settled. To illustrate this sense of "frontier," Maine's border with Canada was not fully complete until the Webster-Ashburton Treaty of 1842. However, southern Maine, with large population centers worth defending such as Portland, was spared the worst of the French and Indian War ravages. As a result, our oldest barns are generally found in southern Maine.

Cumberland and York Counties historically had many farms with accompanying barns, and they still do. The many villages and cities here also have barns within their midst.

York County is Maine's southernmost county and encompasses roughly one thousand square miles. It was incorporated in 1636. Cumberland County is its younger cousin. Incorporated in 1760, the most populated county in our state is just over eight hundred square miles in size.

At a glance:

YORK COUNTY

YEAR	FARMING ACREAGE	NUMBER OF FARMS	AVERAGE FARM SIZE
1940	195, 397	2,249	86 acres
1974	77,7993	459	170 acres
2007	59,335	708	84 acres

Total area: 990 square miles
Population: 197,131 (U.S. census data 2010)

CUMBERLAND COUNTY

YEAR	FARMING ACREAGE	NUMBER OF FARMS	AVERAGE FARM SIZE
1940	223,457	2,937	76 acres
1974	63,753	398	160 acres
2007	51,727	630	82 acres

Total area: 835 square miles
Population: 281,674 (U.S. census data 2010)

As the above statistics show, York County lost significant farming acreage in the thirty-year period between 1974 and 2007. However, the number of farms has actually increased. The situation is mirrored in Cumberland County. Two things have happened: traditional farming operations have given way to numerous and smaller "hobby farms," and development pressures such as sprawl have eroded more of the countryside that has siphoned off chunks of acreage farmers traditionally held. As one struggling farmer in southern Maine puts it, "The biggest crop south of the Androscoggin River is house lots."

But even today, there are still some 1,200 farms in Maine's two southern-most counties. The roots of some of these farms go back to before their county was even incorporated. In fact, York and Cumberland Counties actually have slightly more working farms than that bastion of agriculture known as Aroostook County. However the number of acreage is surely not as favorable.

But more farms generally mean more barns. Southern Maine with its sprawl, shopping malls and highway projects, actually has more barns than the northern portion of the state. Moreover, the number of additional barns within the southern villages and cities pushes southern Maine's numbers even higher. How our southernmost farmers and their barns have managed to survive in an age of development and change is a testament to the fortitude and Yankee ingenuity still firmly entrenched all over our state.

Smiling Hill Farm: An Oasis of Agriculture: Westbrook and Scarborough

Smiling Hill Farm is certainly surviving in the southern part of the state. The Knight family began operations here in 1720, one hundred years before Maine's statehood. In his mid-seventies, Roger Knight, the patriarch of the family, began working full time on this dairy farm at seven or eight years old.

The barn is a giant forty- by one-hundred-foot gambrel-roofed barn dating to 1915. As previously mentioned, the gambrel roof became popular here between the first and second world wars. A gambrel allows a greater hayloft.

Cows were milked in this barn for many years, but it is free of animals today and used for dairy processing, including milk bottling and cheese production. Consumers can buy Smiling Hill Farm products here directly. Today, the farm's cattle are in a modern "barn" that resembles anything but. No hay is stored in this new barn; it has low walls and a slightly pitched roof.

However, with all the changes that have taken place in the last few hundred years, it's the big red gambrel barn that makes this complex a farm. And it's relatively new to the property. With five hundred acres, the Knights were here for roughly two hundred years prior to this barn's construction. With three floors, the building replaces the farm's former barns that were lost to fire in 1915. Most of the buildings, including the old farmhouse, were destroyed when a chimney fire devastated the property.

"They brought in a portable sawmill on top of the hill here and started cutting wood in preparation for the new barn," recalls Knight. "They had the barn up and put the hay in that summer." Replacing the barn was of great importance to the farm, so much so that the new farmhouse did not get built until the following year.

The sun shines bright on this big circa 1915 gambrel barn at Smiling Hill Farm in Westbrook. Gambrels are the third and final generation of traditional wooden barns in Maine.

"Both the barn and the farmhouse were wired for electricity when they were built," said Knight. "But there was no access to electricity." Smiling Hill is on a major thoroughfare that begins at Portland's outer Congress Street. Utility poles went right by the barn along this road back in 1915, but Knight said the utility system was very young and homes had limited access. The farm was finally connected around 1919.

Locals know this area where Westbrook and Scarborough converge as County Road (Route 22). The road heads west out of Portland near the Portland Jetport, the state's largest airport. In fact, Smiling Hill Farm is just three miles away. Retaining five hundred acres for grazing cattle and tree growth in an area full of retail and industrial development has been no small feat.

"We're an oasis of agriculture left in the midst of commercial and industrial development," said Knight. "Back in the '50s when I would visit my sister in Pennsylvania, we went on a trip to New Jersey. Well, here was this nice farm with a chain-link fence and a big factory right beside it. I thought 'that will *never* come to Maine.' But it's here."

"Every bit of land when I was a kid from Brooklawn Cemetery (where Route 22 begins near the Portland Jetport) all the way to here was all farms—every bit of it. They were all small farms, family farms. And they're all gone."

Knight said that barns once littered the landscape. He closed his eyes to stop and count from memory, beginning at Portland's Route 22, the barns of his youth: "One, two, three, four…twelve, thirteen…there were at least fifteen barns between Brooklawn Cemetery and North Scarborough on this road. Many were good-sized barns," he said.

Today, on former farmland at the start of Route 22 on Portland's outer Congress Street is the 120-plus acre Unum property. In the early 1970s, the then Union Mutual moved its corporate headquarters here from downtown Portland. The disability insurer has about three thousand workers here today and is one of the state's largest employers.

West of Unum is the Maine Turnpike and its airport exit sign (Number 46). Then it's a straight line of industrial development toward Knight's farm. Almost directly across the road from Sysco Northern New England's massive refrigerated warehouses is a new sixteen-screen, stadium-style movie theater. There is a slight dip in the road here, and Knight recalled seeing the old-timers cutting ice out of a small body of water—just one mile from the farm.

"Three farms that I know of cut ice there," Knight recalled. "I can remember very vaguely our farm cutting ice there for one or two years when I was a kid."

The ice was stored on the north side of the connecting ell between the Knights' house and the barn. Knight recalled that he and his family milked by hand, and the milk was carried in pails across the barn floor through the grain room, through the shed to a milk tank in the backside of the ell.

"It was a nice milk tank," Knight said. "It was made of galvanized steel and set in the ground about eighteen inches above the floor. On one end, a galvanized box with shelves and a cover on top fit down inside the tank. That was the only refrigeration they had for the house."

The galvanized steel tank measured about seven feet long, five feet wide and five feet deep and was insulated with corkboard. The house received its first refrigerator during the later part or just after World War II. The farm kept its milk in cans set in this early tank, which went from ice as its main means of cooling in the early days, to coils filled with refrigerant.

In the early 1950s, dairy regulations began to change. "Bulk tanks" as the farmers refer to them, were the new innovation. This transformation meant the barn needed to be modified. A new addition for the tank was constructed on the front side of the barn. Double doors were required between the cow tie-up and the new milk room, and the new tank was now cooled by electricity.

Another regulation that, according to Knight, came a little bit later was the addition of a cement floor. A sterile environment was being stressed in the dairy industry at this time and cement floors could be hosed down more effectively than their wooden predecessors. But Knight said the enforcement of cement floors was sporadic at first.

"I had taken over operation of the farm from my father before the cement regulation came," he said. "I installed a cement floor under my tenure, which came eight to ten years after the bulk tank [this was in the early 1960s]."

Knight said that cattle were notorious for wearing out wooden floors in a barn's tie-up area. Every two or three years the top planks needed to be replaced. Knight said elm was used, as was hackmatack or larch, as well as hard pine. However, the life expectancy of the floors was never long.

"With boards, you had a double layer," recalls Knight. "You needed the security of another layer—the boards on top were the wearing boards. With urine and manure getting on and between them, you couldn't keep them clean; it was impossible, even under the best of conditions."

After the cement floor was installed, Knight put in a motorized gutter cleaner for manure handling. Prior to this, the manure was collected by hand and sent down a scuttle, small trap doors located at various points along the length of the tie-up area. Not all farmers, especially small family farms here in Maine, could afford the necessary cement floors and bulk tank upgrades. Many simply got out of the dairy business at this time.

When it was constructed in 1915, Knight said the barn was quite modern for its day. "It was labor efficient," he said. "You got rid of the manure pretty easy, and the hay was all up above. You could get up and pitch hay down to feed the cows."

Today, Smiling Hill has about sixty head of cattle. The largest number Knight ever had was 125, and that number included beef cattle in addition to dairy. Cutting hay and storing it in the barn was a major project. Oxen and horses supplied the labor until the farm got its first tractor in 1950.

"Haying, though laborious as it was, was also enjoyable," Knight recalled. "You weren't under the pressures of today."

Most farms these days usually do two hay cuttings. Prompted by university studies that touted the nutrition of field grass, one cutting now commences in the late spring with another available by mid- to late summer. But Knight recalled a more casual approach.

"Today, it's quality, quality, quality. You've got to cut that hay at the end of May and you've got to get it dry and get it in. And everything is power equipment. But back as a child, yes, they didn't want the hay to get wet, but we weren't really concerned with the maturity of it. They never started haying until after the Fourth of July."

With about sixty head of cattle, Smiling Hill will go through about one hundred tons of hay in a given year. It is no longer kept in the red gambrel barn with its massive hayloft. It's not uncommon to see large, round white bales sitting in a row when passing by a field these days. This is shrink-wrapped hay in one-thousand-pound rolls, and it can stay outside all year; it is no longer stored undercover. No big building, a barn with a traditional hayloft, is required.

As a child, Knight led a cart driven by oxen to mounds of cut grass. With a helper on each side, he and his siblings would pitch the grass into the cart. When it was full, he headed for the barn.

"It was enjoyable," recalls Knight. "You talked, [and] there was camaraderie with everybody."

Knight also recalled the efficiency of the farm's modern gambrel barn in the early days.

"There was no pitching off the hay," Knight said. "We'd fill the middle of that barn with five loads of hay. Right in the middle was where the 'horse fork' was located."

Suspended from the peak of the barn, this grapple on a pulley was often pulled by a horse. But Knight said they used oxen.

"You took a big chunk of hay," said Knight. "I don't know, probably four hundred or five hundred pounds at a whack. It was my job to drive the oxen. I was young; I couldn't even reach the top of their backs. I'd drive them out the barn and up the driveway and father would yell 'HO!'"

The grapple was then released, and the hay dropped into the mow, a storage area usually on the north side of a barn, which is the cooler side. This was preferred because hay is prone to spontaneous combustion. In some barns, the mow went from the floor to the ceiling. But Knight's started on the first floor above the basement. Ten-inch square beams running the width of the barn at the top of the walls were referred to as "the great beams." When Knight was young, loose boards bridged the great beams to make a floor or aisle in the middle of the barn. The hayfork, via the oxen, dumped loads of hay upon this lofty aisle.

"They'd dump that hay on the great beams," said Knight. "There had to be somebody up there pushing the hay off to the guys down below who would rake it into the mow, straighten it out and pack it down."

As the early years ticked by, the Knights figured a way to make this more efficient. A steel-framed ramp was constructed and placed up on the great beams. Oak planks planed smooth on one side were laid on this to make a slide-ramp to direct the hay.

"The hay went up along the track, and when it got to the ramp, my father would dump it down on those slides and whoosh! It went right down into the mow," said Knight. "That saved labor."

Knight said the spontaneous combustion of hay was a real threat. And damp hay was the worst. As grass naturally composts over time, it generates heat. Damp hay can exacerbate the composting action. Countless barns burned from these hay fires. Originally, the barn had a wooden cupola atop its roof that helped the barn breathe. But Knight removed it in the 1960s and added the metal ventilators still in place today.

"Fear of spontaneous combustion was put into me and I held that fear for a good many years," said Knight. "I've reached down into that hay at times and found it so hot [that] you could not hold your hand there. I don't know if it did any good or not, but if you had hay that was questionably dry, you bought salt. You put the hay in and then threw a layer of salt on top. Then some more hay and more salt. They said the salt absorbed the water."

Knight also remembered loading a cart of loose hay in the barn for a delivery to a neighboring farm down the road. This was normally done during the winter. The thought of a youngster in a barn loading a haycart and then driving oxen down County Road is indeed from another time.

Today, Knight has the original 1915 plans for the barn framed on the wall of his house. Drafted by hand on brown kraft stock, the plans, faintly readable, show the barn's anatomy, which is a hybrid of timber and stud framing. Posts and beams with a total of nine bents set on twelve-and-a-half-foot centers make up the frame. Full two- by six-inch studding and rafters on two-foot centers are between each bent. As such, the building is clad in horizontal boarding.

For many years, cows were milked in this barn. In the early 1900s, Knight's father took milk into Portland and sold it for two cents a quart. Then HP Hood purchased Turner Center Creamery in Portland where Hood still stands on Park Avenue today. Knight said the farm sold milk to Hood for over fifty years. When Knight took over from his father in the mid- to late 1950s, he switched to Oakhurst Dairy and sold milk to them for a little over twenty-five years. But in the late 1990s, Smiling Hill Farm brought back the glass bottle. They no longer sell to the big dairies but bottle and sell their

Above: In the late 1990s, Smiling Hill Farm brought back the glass bottle. No animals reside in the big red barn today, which has become a bottling plant and cheese creamery.

Left: Roger Knight, the patriarch of Smiling Hill Farm, stands with a quart of his family's very own product. Like many who grew up on Maine farms years ago, Knight began working here as soon as he was able and has memories of leading oxen into this mammoth barn when he was just seven or eight years old. "I couldn't even reach the top of their backs," he said.

own milk right in their big gambrel barn. The cows are in another building up on the hill.

The big red gambrel has a bottling operation that handles milk of its own, as well as for other farms that are getting into the glass-bottle market. The upper floor of the barn has been completely remodeled into a sterile environment for a cheese operation. Silver Moon Creamery produces artisan cheese where Roger Knight once drove oxen with a cart loaded with loose hay. Cheese is shipped up and down the East Coast and local restaurants purchase it for preparing their dishes.

No doubt, Smiling Hill Farm is a survivor in the southern Maine farming community. Knight's son David is now president of the farm, and the barn—which was so important that it was rebuilt before the farmhouse after a fire claimed everything nearly one hundred years ago—has played a vital role and will continue to be an asset to the family business.

When asked what a barn means to him, Roger Knight said, "It's a way of life; the newness of life. I've delivered thousands of calves in that barn; it's a narrow thread between life-and-death, and I've seen it all. Animals: that's what a barn means to me. Animals."

LEARY FARM: DOING THE RIGHT THING: SACO

At five hundred acres, Leary Farm is the only dairy operation left in Saco today. As recently as twenty years ago, four dairy farms were still selling milk in this city along the Saco River. But like many southern Maine communities, the odds of a farm surviving are not good. Jim Leary, eighty-two years old, is the patriarch of the family and holds the distinction of milking for twenty-four years straight, twice a day, every day, without a break. He turned things over to his son, Tim, some years ago and he said that many farms have gone by the wayside, as well as the barns that went with them. The Saco Museum hosted an exhibit on barns in 2005. At that time, the elder Leary, who is a lifelong resident of Saco, took the opportunity to recount the barns the city once had.

"I counted up the barns that have gone in my lifetime," he said. "Over fifty barns have been torn down or lost (in Saco), and there's been more since then."

Jim Leary started milking cows here sixty years ago and said there were as many farms selling milk as there were barns that have been lost. Most were small operations with roughly a dozen cows or less.

Cattle still reside along Route 1 in Saco. This nearly ninety-foot barn sits on 125 acres of hay field.

"It's hard to believe," he said about the declining number of barns. "I couldn't believe it until I counted them up. There were half a dozen just on Route 1."

Today, Saco's Route 1 is synonymous with the Saco "Auto Mile" and other commercialization. Rows of car dealerships, including Jolly John, were located here. Aquaboggan Water Park is another big attraction for the area. But at 1006 Portland Road (Route 1), just two-tenths of a mile north of Aquaboggan along the four-laned Route 1, you'll find a 125-acre spread with a thirty-six- by eighty-seven-foot barn and its attached farmstead. It is absolutely out of place.

Leary's great uncles, Irving and Merritt Gay, purchased this parcel in 1908. No milking is done here anymore. Instead, about thirty young heifers are kept in the barn and plenty of hay is taken from the fields, which stretch back to the Maine Turnpike. The parcel supports The Leary's main milking operation that is back at their home west of the turnpike on Flag Pond Road. About one hundred head get milked there twice a day. The farmhouse at 1006 Portland Road is rented.

This Route 1 barn holds heifers and hay. As is typical of most barns, the cows are tied along the south side. South-facing windows allow the sun's heat to penetrate during winter. And because Saco borders the coastline, this barn's windows were actually fitted with curtains during World War II. Within a certain distance of the coast all buildings had to be "blacked out" at night so German submarines could not distinguish the outline of American ships against a glowing skyline. However, milking didn't stop because of the war. Leary's relatives pulled the curtains in this barn to disguise their nighttime milking sessions.

A manure shed was constructed at some time along this side of the barn, and the windows were relocated above this. Placed higher than the first floor, these windows still illuminate the cow tie-up below thanks to a floor cutout and a ramp of whitewashed boards that direct the sunlight down to the animals.

The barn is an interesting specimen that helps illustrate the versatility of the New England barn design. Part of a complex of connected farm buildings, this barn is a fine example of our attached architecture that gained popularity here in the mid-nineteenth century. The phenomenon is celebrated in Thomas Hubka's book *Big House, Little House, Back House, Barn.*

At nearly ninety feet, this is a very long barn. New England barns such as Leary's were often enlarged as a farmer prospered over the years. By simply adding bents to the rear of the frame with a full-length center aisle the additional bays were easily accessible for horse and wagon. At some point, three additional bays totaling about thirty-six feet were added to this barn. Leary said this expansion was already in place when his great uncles acquired the property in 1908.

The front of the barn is certainly much older. It's built with reused, hand-hewn timbers. The rear addition exhibits clear differences: sawn timbers and simpler, more modern construction methods including nailed bracing set in a somewhat unorthodox layout are seen. Bracing in the older section is pegged and located in the traditional manner. Rather than being constructed through the hands of an accomplished timber framer, the unconventional workmanship of the rear addition suggests a farmer likely built it to suit his expansion needs.

The point of delineation can be seen at a single post. A top wall plate is evident on the one side, and the bracing is also different. The original construction on the other side is what's often referred to as "dropped girt" or a "connected-girt" system: instead of a top wall plate, the girts connect the frame sections, called bents.

The rafters rest on a top plate in the newer construction, whereas in the former section, short struts bearing on the top connecting girt support the common rafters between each major bent.

Early barn silos were square and housed within the buildings. They often projected above the roofline.

This part also has an interior silo along the north side. The additional bents were not added directly to the silo but begin at the next bay. The whole barn was resided in cedar shingles on this side, and from the exterior, you cannot tell the barn was ever added to.

As previously mentioned, the front section is built of reused timber. Empty mortises are found in unusual locations in most all of the beams, which is a dead giveaway of salvaged timber. It's also a perfect example of the mystery inherent in many of our barns. Where are these timbers from? How old are they? Why did the builders use salvaged timber?

We don't know the answers to these questions directly and can therefore only speculate. Perhaps there was an older barn on site that got dismantled because it didn't fit a new owner's needs. Perhaps a barn in the community was in poor repair and was offered to someone who reused what was still sound. That's the beauty of pegged mortise and tenon joinery: by removing the pegs, the timbers can be separated and used elsewhere. When it comes to barns, recycling is a concept that is nearly as old as the structures themselves. Throughout history entire barns were taken apart, cataloged and loaded onto wagons for reassembly at new sites.

Now in his eighties, Jim Leary has spent more time working in a barn than most folks. For twenty-four years, he never missed a milking, a practice that commenced twice a day, every day—even on holidays.

Though the answers cannot be had with any certainty, what is evident is the fact this barn was built via the new nineteenth-century construction method of "square rule." Housings cut into the bottom of the beams that receive the posts are telltale signs of this construction method. There are no marriage marks pairing timbers together as is often the case in the older practice of scribe rule.

Although no one knows the specific date of this particular barn, the fact that it is paired with a connected farmstead and displays evidence of square rule construction indicates it is from the early to mid-nineteenth century.

The barn's location in prime commercial area meant that it was front and center back in 2003 when a casino referendum was the hot topic here in southern Maine. Developers had their sights on the land directly across the street from Leary for a new racino operation, a combination of racetrack and casino. And they took note of Leary's nicely cleared 125 acres. It was like a blank canvas, perfect for restaurants, shops and hotels. Southern Maine residents may remember the referendum where Scarborough Downs, a popular horseracing track, had to find a new location within five miles to host the proposed racino. The abutting communities of Westbrook and Scarborough were natural alternatives. Developers offered Leary a hefty sum for the property, a sum that was equivalent to $100 for every day the eighty-two-year-old has walked the earth. But Leary refused.

"I didn't like the idea," recalls Leary. "I kind of like this old farm."

It appears some would rather get up and work every day than take the money and lose their heritage.

"Somebody's got to do the right thing," Leary said.

THE HALLS: BIG WHITE BARN A TESTAMENT TO SELF-MADE MAN: WINDHAM

Routes 302 and 202 converge at "The Rotary" at Foster's Corner in Windham, where a big white gambrel-roofed barn serves as a landmark for the area. Beginning near the end of World War II, cows were milked in this barn for about fifty-five years. At one time, Stanley V. Hall was one of the biggest livestock dealers in the state. Mr. Hall passed on February 17, 2012, and was one old-timer I dearly wanted to interview for this book. But it seems I simply waited too late. Stanley Hall may have passed, but his extended family still owns several barns and works hundreds of acres in this area.

Stanley Hall didn't drink or smoke, but he lived a full life. Back in the mid-1940s, at the tender age of twenty-eight, Hall had this thirty-five- by sixty-five-foot barn built. It was a thoroughly modern facility for its time, and additions and upgrades kept it in operation for decades. Empty of animals today, the barn is still used once a week for livestock dealing. Hall's son, Russell, lives nearby and continues the legacy his father built from almost nothing.

Hall was a self-made man in the truest sense. Born in nearby Raymond, both his parents died before he was eleven. Taken in by various relatives in Windham, he began earning his way by breeding and selling rabbits, which got him mobility in the form of a bicycle. By the time he attended Windham High School, milking cows twice a day earned the soon-to-be entrepreneur two dollars and fifty cents a week. At age seventeen, the youngster scraped up enough to buy his first head of cattle. By age twenty-one, he was in the

Ninety-five-year-old Stanley V. Hall (1916–2012) in his Windham barn shortly before he passed away. *Courtesy of George Hall.*

same circles as experienced Portland-based livestock dealers. By the early 1950s, he was considered one of the more prosperous livestock handlers in the state, supplying stock as far away as Massachusetts and Connecticut. The state's largest newspaper took notice.

"He's known throughout the state as a man who can catch the wildest of runaway cows," stated a *Portland Press Herald* article in 1953. "He uses American bull terriers to help corral these critters."

The barn is located in an unlikely spot for a large livestock operation. There is no pasture on the immediate lot, which is mostly ledge with outcroppings of various heights littering the less than one-acre tract. In fact, Hall referred to his operation as Halledge Farm. His Holstein cattle were once registered under this given name.

However, the industrious young farmer made use of the site, which is strategic in its immediate proximity to two major southern Maine highways. For the animals to reach pasture, Hall had a large culvert installed under Route 202 as a tunnel.

"We had an awful time getting the new cattle to get used to going through there," said Stanley's son, George Hall. "Every morning at four o'clock, before milking, dad would have to go out and round up any stragglers."

The barn is built like a fortress, and chock-full of livestock it needed to be. The six-foot-high foundation is poured concrete, sixteen inches thick. At road level, the main floor has sixteen cattle stanchions on each side. The cattle faced inward toward the central aisle. Both sides of the basement were lined with stanchions as well.

"Anywhere you could put a cow, we put a cow," said George.

The *Portland Press Herald* article echoed this. "Stan's main farm—a huge barn contains stanchions for 86 animals—is sort of a Grand Central Station for Maine's traveling cowdom. To the city fellow, it also might appear as a cow store, or a cow replacement agency."

The barn always had cement floors. Poured over boards, the thickness of the cement on the main floor is eight to ten inches, and the depth allowed

Many barns don't have stairways because cattle cannot climb them. Farmers saved on floor space and used permanently fixed ladders for themselves. Ramps were used for cattle. The trapdoor here is where bulls came up from the cellar in the 1950s and were put into a waiting truck to be ferried out to "service calls" for less than five dollars each.

a trough for manure handling. With cattle standing on top of this, one gets an idea of the immense weight the barn had to support. The bulk of the cement floor alone comes in at nearly one hundred tons. Add thirty-two head of cattle at a combined weight of around twenty-two tons, and you've got some significant support needs. This was carried out in the traditional manner of a wood frame. Because it is a modern barn, it does not have a pegged timber frame, but rather a nailed, stud frame. Six- by six-inch interior posts support the first floor, which is made up of beefy three- by eight-inch joists that are spaced sixteen inches on-center. Another interesting detail on the first floor are the feed troughs, which are also concrete and measure three feet high. The walls carry the roof frame entirely, which is an advantage of the then-modern stick-framed gambrel-roof style. No interior posts or beams obstruct the hayloft; the entire roof load is carried directly to the exterior walls. George Hall said this loft can hold 3,500 bales of hay.

Many a man worked in this barn and most of them were local. George, age seventy-four, is the proprietor of a successful John Deere dealership today but lived and worked at this barn until 1961. He remembered taking bulls out for "service calls."

"Three o'clock in the afternoon I'd come home from school, and there'd be a list of places to go," George said. "We'd get three or four dollars each."

Since cattle cannot climb them, there are no stairs between the first and second floors. Instead a ramp with cleats where the animals get footing is in place. George remembers leading two-thousand-pound bulls up the ramp and said they were eager; most knew right where they were heading.

CHAPTER SIX

THE RESTORERS

Resurrecting Our Barns

S olid as they may be, our barns need a little tender loving care now and then. That's where the restorers come in. Roof leaks, poor repair jobs and the general passage of time all take their toll on our barns; they keep the restorers busy. In fact, any restorer worth his salt is likely to have a long waiting list, which can come as a disappointment to many barn owners in need of help, but these folks can take comfort that they've found someone worthy. A good restorer is busy for a reason.

Unlike house carpenters who drape their trucks with all manner of advertising, barn restorers are a little above the fray. They're more like lone wolves; you'll find them driving beefy but ordinary pickups. Often the only marketing they use is word-of-mouth. And they love barns. It's a duty for many. These guys recognize the craftsmanship of long ago and take pride in associating themselves with it. They don't want to see the old barns die. Nailing together walls framed with two- by six-inch lumber doesn't satisfy a craftsman the way splicing a fresh repair into a 150-year-old beam does. They work for the buildings as much as themselves and enjoy the challenges, as every barn presents its own set of problems.

Thankfully, Maine still has an environment to keep the restorers going. There are enough old barns left where a few lucky Mainers can make a career out of putting them back on the level.

Jeremie Berube: Purist with a Passion: Arundel

Some guys collect cars; others collect motorcycles or antique tools. Jeremie Berube not only collects barns, but he also restores them and has several either standing or sorted in racks at his Arundel home. His pride and joy is a late eighteenth- to early nineteenth-century forty- by forty-foot barn that he transported here twenty years ago from Morrill, Maine. Originally, he planned to sell it. He said that it is the first barn that he took down where he finally learned the system of barn "deconstruction." Since then, along with the aid of two cranes, Berube can dismantle a typical barn frame in about two hours.

But it wasn't always that way. In the beginning, Berube learned as he went. Occasionally, he consulted the experts, but most of the time this former house carpenter learned through trial and error.

"I was a carpenter. I am a carpenter," Berube said. "My father was a carpenter. My grandfather was a carpenter. So I was exposed to the trade at a young age. At nineteen, I was a pretty seasoned builder."

Instead of hammering nails every day, Berube ultimately found himself going to college. He returned to Arundel to teach school. But he discovered the pay was less than a good carpenter could make. What's more, Berube always liked working outdoors. "I left the degree behind and went right back to building," he said.

His first deconstruction project was a circa 1790 house, a building he moved to a lot in Arundel and lives in today. He was about to get his first lesson in separating centuries-old timbers. "[After that] I was looking for a barn," he said.

Now in his mid-fifties, Berube has scaled back the amount of barn restoration he takes on, which is a hybrid of demolition, intricate cataloging and aerial acrobatics. It started in the early 1980s. "I was fearless in those days," said Berube. "We didn't have safety harnesses or anything. We made a seat out of a plank and ropes, kind of like a boatswain seat."

A crane hoisted the simple seat up to the high parts of a barn with Berube holding on. He said it was back when you could get away with such tactics on a job site, before inspectors became more commonplace. He learned as he went, and he said it would typically take twelve hours to tear a barn's frame down, which was after all the contents had been emptied and its boarding stripped, a process he said could take nearly a month in itself.

Jeremie Berube stands in one of his beloved barns at his Arundel home. Berube has dismantled, restored and even moved many barns throughout his career.

One day, before he began using cranes, Berube was up in a roof section climbing around a barn's rafters when he suffered a bad fall from the peak.

"I was dismantling his big barn, alone," Berube said. "The entire frame was stripped except for this roof board near the peak. In those days, I walked across the purlins while holding on to an upper one. My wife was nervous; it got dark all around, and there was lightning. She was telling me to come down. Well, I just wanted to get this one piece of wood that was there before the whole frame would be ready to take down. I walked across the purlin, grabbed the board, balancing [myself] and when I pulled the board, the whole purlin came out of its socket. That was it; the weight of it pulled me down."

Berube found himself plunging headfirst toward the barn's floor. He hit on his shoulder and rolled in a thin bed of hay that remained in the barn. He managed to walk away, but the next day he said everything hurt. It was a couple weeks before he returned to the barn. The experience changed him. As soon as he got up to any height he found himself shaking. The whole experience flooded back to his mind. "Once you fall, it changes things," he said.

But he finished the job and said he was soon hooked on his newfound profession. "I remember it was fun," said Berube. "You met old folks in these hidden communities; it was surreal." Since then, Berube has sold entire barns to private customers, historical societies and has completed restorations at the old Shaker community in Alfred.

He remembered being infatuated with Richard Babcock, a well-known authority in barn circles living in Massachusetts who co-wrote the book *Old Barns in the New World*. An expert in the field of barn history, Babcock said that barns are "our strongest link with the colonial past." Berube said he read about Babcock's crew in *National Geographic* and said that was where he came up with his swinging seat idea, after seeing Babcock's group apply a similar setup. Ultimately, in the late 1980s, Berube phoned Babcock to try to learn more, and wound up traveling to Massachusetts to meet the man.

"I was having problems removing pegs; they would oftentimes be swollen after the frame was stripped and exposed to the weather," said Berube. "So I asked Babcock how he did it. He said removing pegs is one of the first things he does—while they're still dry. So now, long before I dismantle a barn, I drive all the pegs out. Otherwise you end up drilling them out. It can be a long process."

It's tips like these that whittled those initial barn deconstruction jobs down from twelve hours to just two. And he learned to label everything. At first, Berube would take photos to assist in reassembly, but he eventually started labeling *every* piece: the posts, the beams, the boards—everything. Little steel tags were marked with a numbering system. That way, instead of being in a random pile when it was time to put the boards back on the frame, they went back on just as they had come off.

Berube loves the old ways of building and has become a skilled stonemason over the years. Berube and his wife keep two horses in their Arundel barn, which sits on an intricately laid bed of stones. Berube learned the method, known as slipform, twenty-five years ago from a colleague who builds stone houses. A wooden form is built, and the stone is laid and mortared inside. It produces a flat face. But Berube modified the approach over the years because he could not see what the finished face looked like until the form was removed. And instead of a smooth surface with the gaps between each stone getting filled with cement, as the form method was designed to produce, Berube likes to keep the mortar set back so that the stone looks almost dry-laid. Instead of using a form, he relies on strings.

Saw marks on lumber cut by a water-powered sawmill. Jeremie Berube is a purist and eschews any circular-sawn wood, a type many in his field label as "modern."

There's a charm to these buildings that Berube is well acquainted with. Like many purists in the business, he likes granite rather than concrete, and the older the wood the better. Because of its age, all the boarding on his barn has vertical saw marks from a water-powered saw mill, but any building he has would likely exhibit them.

"I never keep any circular-sawn wood," he said. "I throw it all out."

THE BARNWRIGHT: RIGHT AT HOME: HARRISON

Scott Hatch studies and restores barns that are within a fifty-mile radius of his home in Harrison. Known as "The Barnwright," he enjoys barns enough that he decided to live in one. In the year 2000, Hatch found an early

Scott Hatch in front of his barn turned home in Harrison. Hatch works full time restoring these buildings.

nineteenth-century barn in the town of Minot, just outside of Auburn. The original owner wanted to put a house where the barn was, which meant the barn was coming down. Though the forty- by sixty-foot structure, which is very tall with twenty-foot posts, presented its challenges, Hatch jumped at the chance to acquire the building. All the sheathing boards had to be stripped, washed and catalogued on pallets. And because it is now insulated and has interior wall partitions, the building has about three barns' worth of boarding throughout. Initially, Hatch scaled things back a bent so that he could have some spare parts, as well as provide a more practical living space for himself, his wife and their little Bichon Frisé.

But living in a barn was not a goal the couple had early on.

"We looked high and low to find a very old and original house we could restore," Hatch said. "But unable to find any, we decided move a barn to this property we had acquired. If you're going to move a building, it's easier to move a barn. Houses just have so much more in them."

The building makes for a charming house. The couple has tastefully incorporated the physical space of a barn—with its high ceilings and open floor plan—with intimate areas such as the front entryway. It's a hand-hewn frame, and all the joinery and pegging is there to see. Catwalks and balconies make up the second floor, and the roof space is open right to the peak. Hatch chose to retain some rustic qualities. There is a rope and hayfork suspended from a track at the peak, and an old beehive up in the rafters makes for a genuine conversation piece.

Modern features such as plumbing, wiring and insulation are handled through a three-inch wall cavity. The roof has two layers of rigid insulation nestled in two by six-inch framing that provides a healthy R-40 rating. The walls are half that, measuring R-20. Heating needs are met through a big wood furnace in the basement, as well as some small monitor space heaters. As such, two layers of boarding with insulation and utilities in between allow for modern amenities while preserving an authentic look both inside and out.

Hatch enjoys New England history almost as much as he does rehabbing our region's barns. He has some theories and interesting insights about Maine and its rural architecture. Originally from Rhinebeck, New York, Hatch began visiting Maine with his parents when he was about nine years old. He moved here permanently in the early 1990s and credits his parents, who did plenty of museum-quality restoration work themselves, with introducing him to older forms of architecture. He grew up around various home restorations.

"My brother and I would get lugged to some restoration site on a weekend, get let out of the car and were left to our own devices to entertain ourselves," said Hatch. "I guess it stuck by osmosis."

After moving to Maine permanently, Hatch did landscaping, excavation and tree work but soon found the field frustrating. When folks want a tree cut or lawn put in, they often want it done as soon as possible. Hatch said he was never more than two weeks out in having work lined up, which can add a lot of anxiety if you're self-employed.

"It soon occurred to me there were a million and one people competing for tree work and light excavation," said Hatch. "But no one was doing what my hobby was, which was restoration work."

One day while he was on a landscaping job, he noticed an accompanying barn in need of repair and suggested that the owner take steps to mitigate its issues before further deterioration ensued. Impressed with Hatch's impromptu assessment, the owner agreed to let Hatch work on the structure.

The owner was pleased, and Hatch soon received a call from another barn owner who had heard of his handiwork.

"I decided to run an ad in the *Portland Press Herald*," Hatch said. "I was broke. It was wintertime and landscaping and tree work were going nowhere. I had $200 to my name and a jar of loose change, so I put a $300 ad in the *Portland Press Herald*, which they let me pay in installments, and I put in the ad and started rolling coins."

Much to Hatch's delight, the ad started paying off. A month later, in the early 1990s, he had $20,000 in deposits from barn owners seeking work and he hadn't lifted a tool. His phone kept ringing. He requested a 10 percent deposit to hold a client's spot in his schedule. Hatch said he hasn't looked back since. When the economy is good, he'll be scheduled two years in advance. When the economy is down he's closer to six months out. That's certainly better than the short two-week lead time he experienced on landscaping and tree work. And he's now doing what he truly enjoys: preserving barns he said can theoretically last one thousand years.

"No one person really owns these buildings," Hatch said. "We all have a tenure where we are in charge of the building for a certain time. But if you think about how many owners a building will survive through, it's amazing. How many different people have had the option to tear their barn down and sell it for salvage, or spend money to fix it? I always tell folks that if they care about their building to try and leave it so that the next owner will be left with a decision that's fairly straightforward. Ideally, the barn will be in good condition and won't require a lot to keep it maintained."

The neglect Hatch refers to is a difficult thing for most barn owners to come to terms with and correct. He says it became much harder to keep these buildings after farming saw its inevitable demise in the early twentieth century.

"Everything changed after the Depression," he said. "World War II and the GI Bill finally ended the Depression. We had a situation where the people were poor, but the government was wealthy. We were able to buy our way out of the Depression by educating our population through the GI Bill; people were able to buy houses. But everything changed. Transportation changed. We had a new highway system; we were wondering whether the Japanese were going to land in Alaska, so we built a road there…we basically came out of World War II with a road system, which aside from highly perishable items such as dairy, largely eliminated the need for farming in New England. You could transport goods here from the Midwest easier than you could produce them here.

"There just wasn't a need for barns—these were industrial buildings for an industry that had failed. It's hard for barn owners to justify spending money on a building they don't need anymore. Dairy still went on, and some folks had the means to keep up their barns, but others didn't. And some folks cared to maintain their buildings while others didn't."

Many clients Hatch speaks with are juggling financial choices. A customer in Gorham had an old twenty-six- by thirty-six-foot English barn that's in desperate shape. The sills were gone, and its posts were basically sinking into the ground. The owners decided it was time to address the building after a severe thunderstorm hit the area and further damaged the building. They're hoping the insurance company will cover the associated costs and the event can serve as a catalyst to address the barn's larger concerns.

But the owners were also trying to put kids through college and have more little ones on the way. What's more, their house needs attention. Hatch said the barn requires upward of $50,000 in repair. He will justify what he can to the insurance company for storm damage, but in all likelihood, the building will get only part of what it needs. It's a common story for many of today's barnfolk.

Hatch has actually been to this barn before. In 2002, his crew fashioned steel brackets, what Hatch refers to as "a long-term temporary repair," to tie some rotten joinery together. These custom brackets are fitted, welded together and attached with lag screws. According to Hatch, they'll last two hundred years if no problems arise (such as a rotten rafter tail, which might be inaccessible to fix without removing the roofing), and he hopes that it is the case until the roof is addressed, at which point the rafter can be properly repaired.

This particular barn is an oldie that dates from the late 1700s. Hatch is familiar with the time period and said that New England, particularly Maine, is unique in how it became a battleground between the French and English. As he's been delving into barns throughout his area, he's proposed an interesting theory about our barns. Hatch said fighting for commodities is nothing new.

"This was the last place on planet Earth where you could build a tall-masted sailing ship from materials available directly inland," said Hatch. "We've got black spruce to the north, white oak to the south and right here in Maine is the pinnacle of the white pine. The French came down from Canada and controlled the black spruce and tried to push the English south to gain power of the white oak. The English landed to the south, had control of the white oak and were trying to push the French north to get control of the black spruce. White oak was frame stock for the ships, the pine was used for masts and the spruce was for decking and planking. Those three species were absolutely necessary for a navy of tall-masted sailing ships."

With the French and Indian War finally settled in 1763, Hatch said northern New England is the first place where French and English timber framing traditions actually began to merge and produce the barns we see here today. English framing is noted for its stark simplicity, while French construction is distinguished by more adornment and complexity. Hatch raises an interesting presumption that would make a fine dissertation thesis for an architectural historian.

Hatch is passionate about his craft, our barns, and the architectural landscape that produced them. Maine can only gain from his enthusiasm. It's likely he'll be bringing our barns back to life—even as homes—for years to come.

Scott Burner and the Barn that Flew: Gorham

Like many barn restorers, Scott Burner came to his craft a bit late in his construction career. He began repairing barns around the year 2000, when he was in his mid-forties, and said a couple of things have worked in his favor over the last decade that have allowed him to focus on barns: people are starting to realize the uniqueness and importance of preserving their old structures, and before the recent downturn, the economy allowed many folks in his part of the state to put money into them.

"Everybody else said tear them down, but I always said I could fix them," Burner said, whose Windham-based company is called S.A. Burner Structural.

Burner grew up in Falmouth and began working in the construction field at an early age. He got his first job at seventeen; it's all he's ever done. Working primarily in residential construction, he built new homes for twenty years. But jacking up buildings of all types is something he's done off and on over time.

Back in 2000, he got a call from someone in Kennebunk. A historic barn was in need of repair. In addition to Burner, three engineers were called in to assess the property.

The Restorers

Barn restorer Scott Burner takes a break on the job site. "Everybody else said tear them down. I always said I could fix them," Burner said.

"One of the engineers said it was beyond saving. Another said to stabilize it and lock it in place," Burner said. The final engineer shared Burner's opinion: jack the building back to level and *then* lock it in place.

"We stood it up straight and cabled it back into position," Burner said. "It was to the owners benefit; he had just purchased the property at a bargain price. He soon resold it at a handsome profit."

This sort of restoration work is certainly physical. Most days, Burner is handling four-foot sections of wooden beams known as cribbing. Barn restorers assemble towers of these as a base for jacking the buildings. He works with sledgehammers and steel I-beams, too, but contrary to these factors, Burner actually prefers working on barns because he said that it's less physically taxing than house carpentry.

"I don't spend the day just driving nails," he said. "It's less repetitive, and I'm not on a ladder all day long."

Burner is a craftsman who draws far more satisfaction in working with the old methods. Cutting two boards and nailing them together is less than stimulating compared to draw-boring a new joint together with pegs.

"You look at a finished repair afterwards and know that will take all forces in all directions," said Burner. "It's not just there until the nail rusts out—it's there. It's going to take some serious force to break it. It's pretty satisfying."

In the summer of 2008, in one community, Burner landed a job that was the talk of the town. On July 18, a severe thunderstorm swept through Gorham with a dreaded microburst. A prominent barn on Route 114 was actually lifted completely off its foundation before crashing down in a pile of rubble. Mike Franck came home from work after his wife called and told him that the sky was getting black. A severe thunderstorm was coming. The early 1900s barn was connected to the house via an ell. Franck and his two dogs were just inside the ell when the wind started screaming.

"I'm in shock at this point because the barn is starting to go straight up," said Franck. "I don't believe what is happening; I just can't comprehend it… the barn is levitating!"

Franck and his two dogs were only just inside the ell, about two feet from the forty-two by sixty-five-foot barn. The dogs were terrified; Franck said time stood still. "I am scared beyond scared."

Though he didn't know it at the time, the difference in pressure caused the eight- by eight-foot cupola on the barn's roof to detach like a cork from a champagne bottle. It flew through the air and landed many yards away, intact, in the middle of the road where it stopped traffic.

"When that came off, it sucked the air right out of the barn," said Franck. "All the walls just imploded."

The barn reached a height of almost four feet before slowly deflating back to the ground. It moved laterally over a total of ten yards. "It didn't crash," said Franck, "It just slowly sat back down."

Franck was utterly paralyzed by what he had seen. Amazingly, he and his dogs were unhurt. The house and the ell remained intact. In fact, Franck had transformed the ell into a haven for his sports memorabilia, all of which remained untouched. His collection of New England Patriots posters from the *Boston Globe* were stapled to the wall and remained motionless during the entire event. So did a collection of nearly fifty baseball hats that were merely hanging on nails. "Not one of them fell off," said Franck.

Bizarre to say the least, Franck and his wife, Sue, now had a pile of debris capped by a big barn roof sitting right next to their house. It wasn't long before they were inundated with phone calls and folks stopping by seeking to salvage the antique barn boards and other material. Franck said many people didn't even ask before pawing over the wreckage. He realized he needed to get it removed quickly. That's when he called S.A. Burner Structural.

The Restorers

"Scott is an excellent worker," Franck said. "We've been blessed to have somebody like him doing this project—someone who cares about what the old barn was and will be saving the timbers to reuse in another structure. That way, the barn will still live on to some extent. Scott knows what he's doing; he's got some good men working with him."

CONCLUSION

We shall not cease from exploration/ And the end of all our exploring/ Will be to arrive where we started/ And know the place for the first time.

These lines from T.S. Eliot's "Little Gidding" sum up my thoughts after deeply researching what was once thought to be a common subject: a barn. The study of barns, what I like to call "barnology," has unlocked doors to many segments of our shared history. I wasn't expecting barns to be a vast subject, but the truth is they are. I am still learning about them and feel there is much yet to discover. Perhaps one day, after all of this exploring, I will truly know barns for the first time...Perhaps.

I am honored to have had the opportunity to write and share this history. Growing up, I had a brief experience with just one barn, and I was almost too young to remember it. In the early 1970s, our family lived in North Yarmouth until I was five years old, and we had a small gambrel-roofed barn where my father kept a few sheep. A very protective and headstrong ram was among them. Sometimes the animal would charge my father when he was in the barn. Dad would often have to grab a hatchet and strike the animal on the forehead with the tool's butt-end. Dad always seemed to sense this before it occurred and would send me to the safety of the hayloft on a ladder that was nailed vertically to the side of the wall. I would watch the goings-on from the safety of this vantage point.

It seems most folks over the age of forty have a story to tell about barns, and it has been very satisfying to document these structures and the associated people. Thankfully, a smattering of young folks still encounter a barn as part of their everyday, too. There's no doubt about it: Barn people are good people.

It was a disappointment that more barns and associated barn folk were not included in this book, and I apologize if you thought your barn would be featured, but I had to adhere to a realistic survey that touched most parts of the state. Perhaps a sequel will be possible one day. Indeed, many more pages of historical and contemporary information on these great buildings could have been written. Barns really are vast subjects.

One of the things I like most about studying barns is the outright adventure of it. Really. When you pull up to a barn you've never seen before your mind can get going. No two are exactly alike. What kind of timbers are pegged within? How are the bents configured? Is the roof made with purlins or common rafters? Do the details of the interior support what is suggested on the outside? Is it one building or two that have been put together? Who worked here? Will there be any markings or joinery that's hardly ever been seen before? Are there secrets here? That's what an adventure really is—not knowing what you'll find.

There is a genuine honesty in old barns; they're real buildings. They can be understood.

I always like to know the motivations for things and, from time to time, have tried to pinpoint what it is that draws so many of us to barns. People truly harbor a romantic affinity for these buildings, more so than homes, it seems. What is it then that fascinates us about these common structures? Though I'm still formulating an answer to this apparently vast question, I have a bit to offer: old barns with their stout timbers evoke a feeling of permanence, strength and protection, something that is all too absent from modern, stick-framed structures of plywood-thin walls and vinyl siding.

Subconsciously, we recognize and understand the enduring nature of trees. Hand-hewn posts and beams are not too far removed from these origins. But there's more to a barn than just the posts and timbers. For a child, a barn can be outright freedom. Unlike the confines of a house where nineteenth-century children were not allowed to play ("roughhouse"), the barn is a place to play hide and seek, to swing on ropes, to jump into mounds of hay or to walk a death-defying scamper across a great beam. Many senior citizens speak fondly of playing in barns as children. It was a place much larger than the house with its associated guidelines that thankfully didn't apply.

But for the carpenter, old barns hold absolute mystery. Hand-hewn frames are unlike any building a carpenter contends with today. Modern lumber is true and square; power tools easily make square cuts, making it all too easy to "nail-up" a square frame. Today's carpenter would surely be lost if given uneven timber and simple hand tools and asked to cut joinery for a level, plumb and square frame. It is simply a completely different animal. The two disciplines overlap far less than one would imagine.

The carpenter of old knew how to use an ax and which trees to select. He also was conditioned to trust what had come before; he did not need an engineer's calculations of snow load and other such particulars. Joinery was a school with literally centuries of trial and error "built" into it.

There were standards. Barns are made from eight- by eight-inch timbers, not because that's what size trees were available to hew but because that's what had been thoroughly tested. This size allowed posts to remain rigid with mortises cut into them; it's what allowed two-inch tenons–the standard in old frames—to effectively work. From at least medieval times until about the mid-nineteenth century, the carpenter of old was designer, builder, engineer and architect all rolled into one. With the osmosis of the industrial age, these professions split into separate camps, and to this day, it is typical for builders and architects to somewhat dislike one another since they naturally come up through different classes of society. Carpenters feel architects and engineers lack hands-on experience with building materials, while architects and engineers feel carpenters lack the ability to predict and factor in stresses and design considerations. Both camps are largely correct in their position. Unlike a common blue-collar, pickup truck–driving carpenter of today, who is seen as only slightly skilled, the joiner of old belonged to a respected artisan class and was valued for his knowledge and important service to the community. The Amish still bestow such distinctions.

Surveying the different parts of the state for this book has been a real honor and a pleasure. Maine is a diverse place with the barns as different as the many localities. Through "barnology," it was learned that settlements are generally older in the southern part of the state, while traditions persisted in the isolated eastern and northern sections. Finding hand-hewn frames in circa 1900 barns in Aroostook County was a surprise at first, since this is almost never found on southern Maine's barnscape. By the early 1900s, barns in southern sections were built with sawmilled timber. Mortise and tenon joints, if found at all, were often secured with nails instead of pegs. It simply illustrates there are many factors to consider when trying to date a barn. Location is just as important as the type of construction or saw mark discovered.

Again, many things were learned through the course of this study. One of the things I found most intriguing was the fact that Maine was never considered great farmland, for farmers have struggled here since the beginning, and people were drawn to lumber and fish industries instead of farming. But probably the most notable discovery of all this "barnology" is the English tying joint and its half millennium–long tenure among those of English ancestry. This was a facet unknown to me in the beginning, and I feel a real duty to disseminate this awareness, which has remained too obscure for too long. In my mind, an "ETJ" should be reason enough to get a barn on the *National Register of Historic Places*, since it is one of the last readily observable details "tying" New England to the Old World.

What was also an eye-opener, even for a native Mainer, was to learn just how English Maine was in the early days. It's odd that one would discover such things through barn research, but you can't help running into it. This truly was "New England."

A chapter in *A History of Maine Agriculture 1604–1860* by Clarence Albert Day (1954) reads:

> *Maine people were deeply rooted in the British Isles. The vast majority were of pure English blood, or descendants of Scotch-Irish immigrants from Northern Ireland. Minor groups included the remnants of two Indian tribes, the Penobscot and the Passamaquoddies; the French along the St. John and the descendants of a small colony of French Huguenots who had settled at Dresden; and the Germans in and about Waldoboro, whose ancestors had been introduced by Samuel Waldo to settle there. As to religion the entire population was Protestant, except the Madawaskans, the Indians, and a handful of Irish Roman Catholics at and near Whitefield—in all not one per cent of the population.*

In certain respects, such a homogenous population continues to exist in Maine today. In 2009, a *Bangor Daily News* article reported national census figures showing Maine as "the oldest and whitest state in the nation." Vermont is second; the two states have traded for first place here in recent years. Maine was 95.3 percent white in 2009, while the national average was 66 percent.

Indeed, tradition still runs deep in the Pine Tree State. Our barns have and should continue to be central figures in the proud and hard-earned story of Maine. If nothing else, peeking into our barns can help us truly "know the place for the first time."

GLOSSARY OF
BARN-RELATED TERMS

What You Need to Know from A to Z

Adze: A long-handled, edged tool typically used to dress or finish hand-hewn timber.

Aisle Post: primary vertical member bordering either side of a barn's main aisle; can run from floor to tie beam, or floor to roof rafter.

Bay: A cross section of a barn, typically between and defined by a pair of bents.

Beam: A primary horizontal structural member that spans a gap and supports a floor, roof or other structure above.

Beetle: A large wooden sledgehammer used to pound joinery together.

Bent: A crosswise-timber truss in a barn's framework. Old barn raising photos will typically show many workers lifting a bent into position.

Brace: sloping secondary member that connects and keeps other members from racking out of position.

Broadaxe: An edged tool typically used to hew logs; a wide-bladed axe head with a single bevel and mounted to an offset handle.

CARPENTER'S MARKS: Also known as marriage marks. Typically seen in scribe-rule framing, roman numerals or other symbols are chiseled into timbers that must be paired together at assembly.

CIRCULAR-SAWN: Refers to arced-shaped saw marks left on wood by a circular saw (a round, disc-shaped saw blade).

CONNECTED-GIRT FRAME: A barn frame characterized by the lack of a continuous (or any) wall top plate. Bents are tied together with girts that are typically dropped eight to twenty-four inches from top of post.

CRIBBING: Alternating short timber stacked in a four-sided framework to support a section of barn for repairs.

CUPOLA: A wooden, roof-mounted vent often with a weathervane attached at its top. A barn can have one or several on its roof peak.

DRAW-BORING: A technique used with tapered pegs where mortise and tenon peg holes are offset. The joint is drawn tight upon driving peg.

ENGLISH TYING JOINT: Area of barn frame where rafter, tie beam and wall plate converge over a jowled (flared) post.

GABLE ROOF: The most common style of barn roof. Each side and slope is symmetrical and forms an "A" shape.

GAMBREL ROOF: A symmetrical roof style with two slopes per side. The lower slope is steeper than the upper. Term originates from similarity of a horse's rear leg joint.

GIRT: A horizontal member in a frame, usually in a wall and used to connect posts.

HAND-HEWN: Refers to timber squared by hand with an axe.

HAYMOW: A section of barn where hay is stored; different from a *hayloft*.

JOIST: Horizontal floor or ceiling framing member typically spaced at equal distances. It provides support and nailing surface for floorboards and/or ceiling material.

JOWLED POST: A post with a flare at its top that provides increased surface area for intersecting joinery. These posts are typically hand-hewn rather than sawn. The tree is inverted so that the wider butt end becomes the post's top.

MORTISE: The female component of a mortise and tenon joint; a hole or slot in a timber's face that typically accepts a tenon.

PEG: A wooden fastener that is typically pointed and fastens timbered joinery (e.g. mortise and tenon, lap, etc.).

POST: A vertical support in a frame that supports a beam, rafter, plate or purlin.

PURLIN: (major) a primary horizontal member that supports roof rafters at their midsection; (minor) a secondary horizontal member in a roof that supports vertically applied roof boards.

RAFTER: A sloped-supporting roof member that runs from the roof ridge down to the eaves.

SASH-SAWN: Refers to straight "up-and-down" saw marks left on wood by a sash saw.

SCRIBE RULE: A layout and assembly method where intersections of members are literally scribed into the wood. Each piece of the frame is custom fitted and marked for assembly.

SCUTTLE: A trapdoor or plank in a cattle tie-up area where manure is dropped into a cellar or pit.

SHIP'S KNEE: A continuous piece of wood that forms an approximate right angle and is used for bracing in barns. Ship's knees are typically made from a stump or tree-branch section and are commonly used in traditional shipbuilding.

SQUARE RULE: A layout and assembly method employing the theory of interchangeable parts. Unlike its older counterpart, the scribe rule, the final dimensions of many frame pieces are predetermined and not custom fit.

TENON: The male component of a mortise and tenon joint. A tenon typically protrudes and has been reduced in size to fit into a mortise.

TIE BEAM: A beam that keeps walls from spreading outward under the load of a pitched roof. It is often the bottom horizontal member of a roof truss.

TRUNNEL: An oversize wooden peg typically fashioned by hand and associated with shipbuilding as well as bridge building. The name is a corruption of "treenail."

DIAGRAMS AND DRAWINGS:
A VISUAL PERSPECTIVE

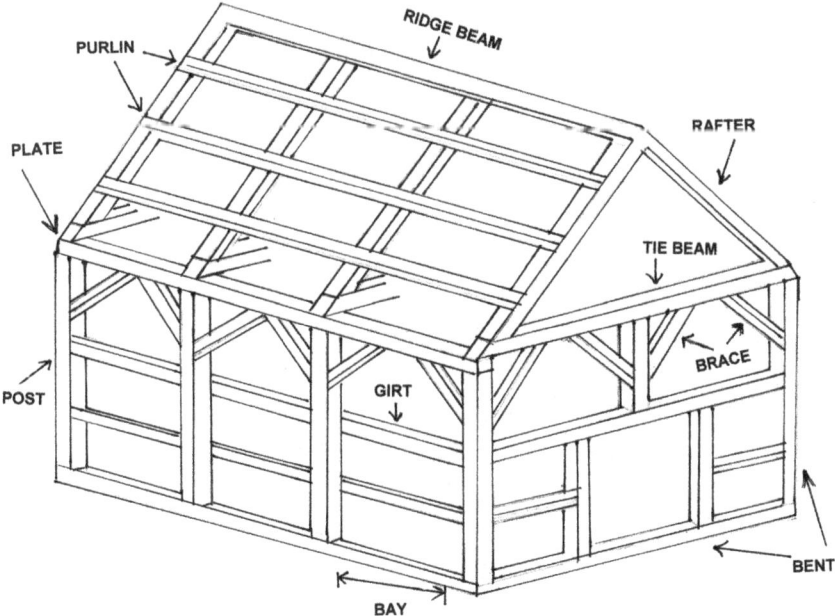

The various frame parts on a typical barn.

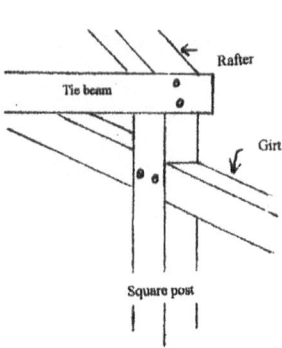

Dropped" or " Connected Girt" framing with square post

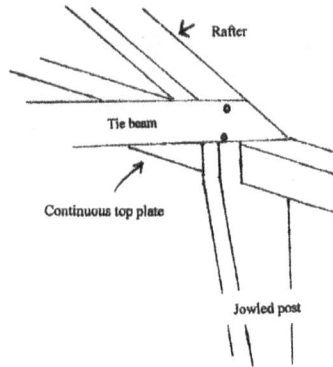

Traditional "English Tying Joint" with jowled post

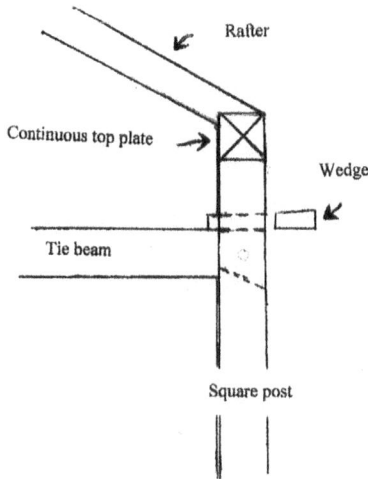

"H-bent" Configuration;
Tie beam is dropped and sometimes dovetailed & wedged in place

The three most common post and bent configurations of barns in Maine: *Top left*: Dropped- or connected-girt framing with square post. Note configuration has no top wall plate. *Top right*: Traditional English tying joint with jowled post, the origins of which go back to thirteenth-century England. *Bottom*: "H-bent" construction with square post. The tie beam is dropped and sometimes displays a half-dovetailed tenon that is wedged in place. An oversized mortise is required for tenon insertion.

Close-up of carpenter's or marriage marks, indicating the scribe-rule framing technique on a mid-1800s Harpswell barn.

ABOUT THE AUTHOR

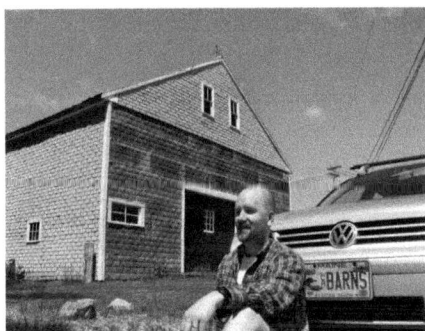

Don Perkins, a self-described "barnologist" and resident of Sebago Lake, Maine, has a passion for barns. Don speaks at area historical societies and leads barn tours. He is a former carpenter and woodworker with a longtime interest in timber framing and is a current member of the Timber Framers Guild. Don traveled statewide in order to survey the people, history and craft of Maine's barns, placing the findings and photos here on the printed page.

A freelance writer since 2005, Don first penned a series on local barns in 2007–8 for a Gray–New Gloucester weekly publication. The series garnered much interest and ran for twenty weeks. Another barn column appeared in the *Advertiser Democrat* in Norway, Maine, for a year and a half. For seven years, he wrote a weekly column on people and events for the *Portland Press Herald*.

Don is available for barn research, tours and speaking engagements. He can be reached at www.ourbarns.com.

www.ingramcontent.com/pod-product-compliance
Lightning Source LLC
Chambersburg PA
CBHW070345100426
42812CB00005B/1431